I0428357

Contents

Executive Summary

The OSS Model and the Future of the SOF Warrior Seminar, 11-12 January 2011, MacDill Air Force Base, Florida

It has been some 70 years since the Office of Strategic Services (OSS) quietly came into being as a small, nearly invisible, Washington, D.C.-based organization whose unique capabilities and strategic reach resulted in decisive outcomes within World War II European, Chinese, Southeast Asian and other theaters of operations. Today the record of the OSS survives as far more than a topic of historical curiosity. As a result of its dramatic successes and failures, the OSS has developed a legacy of mission accomplishment that survives as a practical touchstone for the (SOF) Warriors of the 21st century.

In fact, the OSS Model continues to provide fresh insights and practical relevancy to the concept of persistent engagement as practiced by today's United States Special Operations Command (USSOCOM). In speaking about the OSS veteran, a contemporary Special Forces officer observed that ―we must understand who he is, not just what he did."

As part of his Commander's Guidance for 2011, then USSOCOM Commander Admiral Eric T. Olson directed that a study be undertaken to address if and how the OSS Model could serve as a source of inspiration to incorporate into USSOCOM efforts to select, organize, resource, and develop authorities for SOF of the future. Specifically, the study was intended to identify ways to promote agility in the command through leveraging the OSS selection process, modeling its streamlined organizational structure, using the OSS simplified resourcing authorities, and adapting its charter and authorities to conduct seamless intelligence and operations. Admiral Olson highlighted the OSS attributes of expertise, ability to leverage networks and creativity to guide JSOU's efforts.

The Joint Special Operations University (JSOU) engaged selected members of the USSOCOM Staff, Office of the Secretary of Defense, Central Intelligence Agency, U.S. Army Special Operations Command, U.S. Army John F. Kennedy Special Warfare Center and School, and the OSS Society to assist in the development of recommendations for Admiral Olson's review. JSOU organized the participants into four study groups addressing both OSS and USSOCOM approaches to the Selection, Organization, Resourcing, and Authorities of SOF. The study groups began their discussions following the Innovation Workshop conducted at USSOCOM on 16 November 2010. Three principles guided the proceedings of that Innovation Workshop and subsequent discussions: Understand the nature of the operational environment; recognize the need for a small, innovative footprint for forces engaged within the operational environment; and ensure sufficient flexibility in the relevant authorities to allow for the innovation necessary within the operational environment.

These principles were amplified by the following thoughts: The expertise of the OSS allowed members of the organization to understand the operational environment; to understand the language and culture; and to understand the nature of the enemy's purpose or at least their objectives. The OSS recruited regional experts to apply their skills as operators and to be the ―reach back" for additional resources and knowledge as needed. The SOF community has similar requirements today, and USSOCOM expects current and future SOF warriors to have the same level of expertise as the OSS warrior. The OSS members' ability to leverage a multitude of personal and professional networks was instrumental to their operational success. The OSS leadership recruited its personnel by relying on contacts with business leaders, social elites, university academics, and other professionals. Those operators sent overseas leveraged the networks within their areas of operation to work against enemy networks. Today's SOF warrior is not as focused on or as skilled in leveraging or exploiting networks for a variety of reasons, including the relative lack of advanced language and cultural awareness skills.

Creativity enables the innovation that is required during operations for successful outcomes. While expertise and leveraging can be taught or developed, creativity is a trait not easily replicated. It is, however, a character trait expected in SOF warriors as they are placed in situations where creativity means the difference between success and failure.

Each of the workgroups presented their recommendations and thoughts to those attending the seminar on *The OSS Model and the Future of the SOF Warrior* on 11-12 January 2011. As a result of those contributions and subsequent discussion, the following recommendations, organized by issue, emerged for developing SOF that demonstrate flexibility and are able to adapt to the changing security environments SOF encounters.

Selection Process

Seek authorities for USSOCOM J-1 to monitor, influence and coordinate all personnel issues, including recruitment and selection, related to all of SOF and not just limited to USSOCOM command and staff as is the current situation.

Expand the Human Capital Plan so that it not only addresses the rapid acquisition of new expertise, but one that exploits existing skill sets and experience residing in persons now retired from the active force, but still available through the concept of ―SOF for Life."

Modify and strengthen the Human Capital Plan to manage more effectively the career tracks for SOF personnel and to develop further and harness the regional, cultural, and linguistic expertise of both organic SOF operators and personnel with service-provided capabilities.

Establish a selection process for non-operator and service-provided capabilities (formerly referred to as "enablers").

Build and maintain a SOF personnel pool that is made up of varied cultural backgrounds and races, that are capable of mastering different languages, and that are adept of navigating cultural and ethnic boundaries.

Extend, expand and strengthen the current Military Accessions Vital to National Interest (MAVNI) Law—similar to the Lodge Act—to encourage the recruitment of foreign nationals or other recent immigrants seeking U.S. citizenship through military service.

Expand recruitment efforts in specific ethnic neighborhoods and enclaves in the United States where immigrant groups have settled.

Review existing USSOCOM programs against OSS practices to attract native speakers and to expedite procedures for obtaining security clearances in order to bring their skill more rapidly into the fight.

Make even greater use of a common SOF assessment process by having candidates complete a battery of psychological and aptitude assessments to determine the specific characteristics required for success in today's SOF.

Apply a 360-degree feedback mechanism as part of the assessment process to add to its effectiveness in measuring the "whole man" (similar to the OSS process).

Continue to strengthen recruitment efforts through the use of current SOF personnel to "get the word out" to current service members, those who are considering joining the services, and those who possess the attributes or specific skill sets that will contribute to the SOF mission.

Organization

Compare and contrast OSS Morale Operations with current Military Information Support Operations (MISO) and Civil Affairs (CA) structures to determine ways to increase team integration from planning to execution and subsequent synchronization with SOF ground units to develop a regional orientation.

Introduce on-the-job training approaches to increase CA skills for those members engaged in sewage treatment plant, oil field operations, and other functions, similar to the training concept employed by SOF medics.

Study the OSS employment of women in operational positions with respect to the current gender restrictions on all SOF organizations to determine if any modifications can be applied to today's Combat Support Team (CST) approach.

Review Security Assistance Force (SAF) structures employed by forward-deployed SF battalions to address the concept of "bolt-ons" to increase capabilities and unit cohesion in regional operations.

Update Interagency Task Force (IATF) plans to determine other ways to leverage economic tools ("follow the money") in the current fight against terrorists and their networks by considering how the OSS employed its economic warfare capabilities.

Resourcing

Accelerate SOF-to-Service common acquisitions to reduce duplicative acquisition costs and increase economies of scale.

Establish a SOF integrated Research and Development battle laboratory to develop Irregular Warfare capabilities and other relevant technologies.
Develop ways to better leverage and manage existing commercial R&D capacities and products.

Further investigate the ability to concentrate SOF resources on select persistent engagement activities to respond more effectively within the international security environment.

Authorities

Pursue changes in Department of Defense (DOD) oversight; manage USSOCOM more as a "Special Capability" with appropriate funds as contrasted to a service-like entity, to streamline the numbers of reviews, reports, and decision layers.

Request Congressional authority for USSOCOM to operate with appropriate funding similar to the OSS's unvouchered funds to reduce overhead and increase USSOCOM's ability and flexibility to meet urgent needs.

Educate relevant USSOCOM staff on Section 1206/1207/1208 funding and authorities, thus enabling a more rapid ability to support partner nations. Seek legislative support to expand and extend Section 1208 beyond Fiscal Year 2013.

Increase and clarify the appropriate authorities enabling USSOCOM roles in intelligence operations.

The Authorities Group recommended seeking senior contract status at SES level for needed civilian expertise instead of a senior-level direct commission capability. For the ability to direct commission at any rank, USSOCOM must obtain individual service agreements from the appropriate service to bring individuals on active duty as commissioned officers. Furthermore, these commissions would most likely require staff or non-line officer status. USSOCOM is interested in the authority to grant a uniformed commission at senior level rank (O-6) and above for specific purposes and limited durations to meet specific urgent SOF needs. Refine USSOCOM roles and responsibilities in synchronizing plans for global operations, and develop Joint SOF Doctrine to support such efforts.

Summary

It is important to remember that the OSS was, in essence, an experiment that lasted only a few years. The fact that the OSS did not reach full maturity and did not become constrained by predictable bureaucratic limitations provides an important record of both success and failure. This serves as a reach back as to how contemporary and future SOF can learn from and exploit the OSS legacy. These recommendations are intended to provide SOF Warriors with an agile, sustainable, and effective ―Way Ahead" to confront the inevitable uncertainties of the evolving international security environment.

Overview

Admiral Eric T. Olson, then United States Special Operations Command (USSOCOM) Commander, directed a study be conducted to address one of his concerns on the future of Special Operations. He expressed numerous times that the World War II-era Office of Strategic Services (OSS) may be a source of inspiration to address his questions on the future of Special Operations. The Joint Special Operations University (JSOU) received the task in late 2010 to lead a study and it engaged selected members of the USSOCOM Staff, Central Intelligence Agency (CIA), United States Army Special Operations Command (USASOC), The United States Army John F. Kennedy Special Warfare Center and Schools (USAJFKSWCS), and the OSS Society to assist in the development of recommendations for the USSOCOM Commander's consideration. In addition three respected historians served as academic advisors to the project: Dr. Nancy W. Collins, Columbia University; Dr. Troy Sacquety, USASOC historian; and Mr. Rob Townley, OSS Society.

This directed study began in earnest with a one-day OSS Innovation Workshop on 16 November 2010. It was attended by selected USSOCOM staff members and led by JSOU senior fellows to answer predetermined questions on OSS practices and applications in four specific areas of interest for the USSOCOM Commander: Selection, Organization, Resourcing, and Authorities. The workshop participants, along with select participants from the Special Operations Forces (SOF) community participated in four study groups and were tasked to research each of the commander's areas of interest, answer specific questions developed for each of the four sections, and make recommendations. This endeavor culminated with a JSOU sponsored symposium ―The OSS Model and the Future of the SOF Warrior," from 11 to 12 January 2011, at MacDill Air Force Base, Florida, where a comprehensive review of the study groups' findings were discussed and debated, and further recommendations made.

It is also noteworthy to mention that this directed study was preceded by a two-day symposium conducted by JSOU and the OSS Society in November 2009 titled ―Irregular Warfare and the OSS Model," in which OSS veterans were interviewed and their accounts recorded. Three persistent themes from these events, previous studies, and research on the OSS were identified: the necessity to *understand* the operational environment; a penchant for *innovative* organizational design including small footprint for operations; and the requirement for *flexible application of authorities* to adapt to conditions in theater. These themes were embraced by the USSOCOM Commander and underpinned the research and seminar discussions through January 2011. It should also be noted that research focused on U.S. Army Special Forces since this community comprises the principal land component to Special Operations and historically draws inspiration from the OSS experience. All research was completed using unclassified or declassified documents and interviews. A considerable amount of data from the National Archives was made available to the study and seminar participants by a member of the OSS Society.

The bulk of this report is made up of the four study groups' reports that summarize responses to questions developed by JSOU for the four areas of interest directed by the USSOCOM Commander. Each study group's summary is presented in the context of the three themes identified earlier and highlighted at the November 2010 Innovation Workshop. Recommendations drawn from the study and the January 2011 symposium are presented in Annex A. A synopsis of the After Action Report from the Innovation Workshop is enclosed in Annex B for context. Finally an OSS reading list is included in Annex C.

The Selection Study Group dealt with not only the review of the current USAJFKSWCS process for selecting Special Forces candidates, but also the similarities to the CIA and that of the OSS. It also looked at the OSS's ability to directly commission experts into the OSS. This was of great interest to the USSOCOM Commander to have similar authorities. Another area of interest for this group was the issue of language skills. This question dealt with both the ability to learn languages and how to recruit fully qualified native speakers into the services. USAJFKSWCS and members of the CIA were participants in the study and contributed with firsthand knowledge on their selection process. It should also be noted that although USSOCOM is a joint organization, the Selection Study Group focused on Special Forces as the cornerstone. U.S. Army Special Forces is the principal land component to Special Operations historically and this study uses it as a common reference point.

The Organization Study Group dealt with the areas of current structure, command and control, and comparing them to the OSS structure. This group also looked at the Understand and Small Footprint Themes to develop their recommendations on the future of Special Operations. A separate USSOCOM innovation workshop team (SOF Operator 2020) was also was consulted for input. Additionally, the USSOCOM Interagency Task Force (IATF), simultaneously conducted a study on OSS Morale Operations, and was engaged for their input.

The Resourcing Study Group dealt with funding, education and material support. This group examined the historical records of the OSS and Special Forces to determine the cost of developing the organizations for manpower and material.

The Authorities Study Group investigated the OSS authorities, the enabling authorities for the CIA and USSOCOM to determine where they disconnect and what may be required to support USSOCOM for the future. This study, probably more so than the others, was limited by use of only unclassified information.

Methodology

JSOU reached out to OSS veterans, academics, and practitioners of the special operations profession to conduct this short study. A data base on the OSS was made available, as were the records under the control of the USSOCOM Historian's Office. Components of CIA provided limited information because of the unclassified nature of this project. The USSOCOM U.S. State Department representative provided details on the use of selected hiring authorities to assist in the effort as well. The OSS Society facilitated access to veterans, who openly provided comments, participated in the review of the material, and attended the January 2011 symposium.

This short study reflects a series of complex issues that have a long history in constantly changing operational environments. The current and future realities have transformed from wars between nation-states to violent conflict between loosely configured groups of terrorists, or violent extremist organizations with elements of criminal groups spanning the world. JSOU assembled this document as a set of findings supported by data to serve as the basis for further discussion and possibly a more focused study at the classified level for USSOCOM to consider. Each of the 4 sections of this report were intended as standalone documents, and the sections collectively contribute to the comprehensive review of potential applications of OSS-inspired models for consideration by U.S. Special Operations Forces.

Background

The Office of the Coordinator of Information (COI) and later the Office of Strategic Services (OSS) was established in 1942 during World War II (WWII) under the direction of Major General William J. —Wild Bill" Donovan to develop strategic intelligence and carry out unconventional warfare. An enigmatic leader, General Donovan was revered by his troops; however was also known for his poor managerial skills and his disdain for the administrative. In contrast to the rapid growth of the OSS during the war and despite Donovan's appeal to retain a peacetime intelligence capability, the OSS was quickly dissolved by an executive order signed by President Harry S. Truman in 1945. Activities and components of the OSS were hurriedly divided between the State and War Departments shortly after the conclusion of the war.[1]

---

[1] Michael Warner, —An End and a Beginning" *The Office of Strategic Services: America's First Intelligence Agency* (e-book). Center for the Study of Intelligence, Central Intelligence Agency, 15 March 2007; available at https://www.cia.gov/library/center-for-the-study-of-intelligence/csi-publications/books-and-monographs/oss/art10.htm; accessed December 2010.

In 2011, the force structure for USSOCOM was approximately 55,007 uniformed personnel and approximately 6,467 civilians. In Fiscal Year (FY) 2011 the USSOCOM estimated budget for operations and maintenance (O&M) was approximately $3.95 billion.[2] In comparison, the OSS expended $43 million in FY 1945, and spent almost $135 million over its four-year existence (equivalent to $1.1 billion in 2007). The OSS at its zenith was made up of almost 13,000 personnel, with approximately one quarter of that civilian.[3]

In his farewell address to his subordinates, General Donovan congratulated the OSS for being —an experiment to determine whether a group of Americans constituting a cross-section of racial origins, of abilities, temperaments and talents could meet and risk an encounter with long-established and well-trained enemy organizations."[4] The efforts and exploits of the innovative and clever men and women of the OSS enabled the Allies to exploit economy-of-force missions throughout Europe and the Pacific theaters through their small footprint, intelligence-gathering, and advisory methodologies. Today's American SOF, in particular Army Special Forces, assert their heritage and lineage back to the OSS. USSOCOM also acknowledges the inspiration of the OSS in its logo; a gold lance head referred to as —the tip of the spear."

---

[2] Fiscal Year 2011 Budget Estimates, U. S. Special Operations Command (USSOCOM), USSOCOM 654, February 2010; available at http://comptroller.defense.gov/defbudget/fy2011/budget_justification/pdfs/01 _Operation_and_Maintenance /O_M_VOL_1_PARTS/SOCOM_FY11.pdf; accessed October 2011.

[3] Michael Warner, —What was OSS?" *The Office of Strategic Services: America's First Intelligence Agency* (e-book). Center for the Study of Intelligence, Central Intelligence Agency, 15 March 2007; available at https://www.cia.gov/library/center-for-the-study-of-intelligence/csi-publications/books-and-monographs/oss/art03.htm; accessed December 2011.

[4] Michael Warner, —An End and a Beginning." *The Office of Strategic Services: America's First Intelligence Agency* (e-book), 2007.

Selection

This section summarizes research and findings on the OSS approach toward personnel selection and assessment, including the establishment of the first psychological assessment program. It will highlight the current approach taken by U.S. Special Forces (SF) and the CIA toward personnel selection and offer some recommendations for application as it relates to the future of U.S. Special Operations Forces. Judgments expressed are drawn from reading OSS-related literature, discussions with military officers and civilian leaders from the office of the Deputy Assistant Secretary of Defense for Special Operations and Low Intensity Conflict (DASD/SO/LIC), the USAJFKSWCS, the USASOC, and current and former officers at the CIA. A set of Study Questions were developed to guide and trigger discussion intended to yield concrete recommendations. Colonel Louie M. Banks, the USASOC chief of psychological evaluation, offered his personal insight in the selection and assessment process for OSS personnel and Army SF and was a key contributor to this group in answering the study questions.

What are the criteria used for selection in the CIA (Clandestine Service and paramilitary officers) and Special Forces today? How do they compare with and how are they different from selection for duty with the OSS?
Current SOF and CIA recruiting processes are derived largely from the OSS and its processes. They include strong recruiting from a variety of sources, psychological assessments, and evaluations to determine mental and physical agility and toughness. The OSS recruited from all ranks and strata of U.S. society. They relied upon personal recommendations and social networks to recruit the best of the brightest, including many captains of industry and others steeped in knowledge of technology. They also recruited first- and second-generation Americans from mostly European ethnic groups to make maximum use of their vast native language capability and cultural awareness.

In its first year of operations OSS leadership became concerned with reports from the field of OSS agents' inability to adapt to the challenging environments they were operating in despite many having apparent cultural and language connections. A psychological-psychiatric assessment entity with a formal assessment role was established partially based on the model used by the British,[5] and staffed by respected

---

[5] Louie M. Banks, "The History of Special Operations Psychological Selection," (Fort Leavenworth, KS, 1995), reprinted in *Psychology in the Service of National Security*, edited by Dr. A. David Mangelsdorff, 2005, http://users.idworld net/dmangels/apampsy.htm, accessed December 2010.

psychologists throughout the U.S. [6] Over 5,000 OSS candidates were screened and assessed in the year and half that followed, and according to Colonel Banks, this was the precursor to modern day assessments used in civilian assessment centers and by Army SOF.[7]

U.S. Army Special Forces were first assigned under the Psychological Warfare Center at Ft. Bragg, North Carolina. SF teams were originally intended to counter the Soviet Union and its proxies in Europe by conducting guerrilla warfare and sabotage during the Cold War. Its team-centered organization and operating tactics techniques and procedures (TTP) were modeled after the 1st Special Service Force, the OSS, and other specialized units during World War II (WWII). SF numbers and its missions were later expanded by President Kennedy's personal support in the early 1960s to include counterinsurgency.[8] The yearlong SF training process had a high attrition rate, and with the increased through-put required during the Vietnam conflict, assessment and selection issues arose.

The use of psychological assessment as part of the SF selection process was eliminated later during the Vietnam War and was not used again until 1988. According to Colonel Banks it has now become engrained as part of the formal assessment program, and as of December 2010, approximately 59,404 soldiers have been screened for duty. ―Army SOF psychology has greatly expanded to where it currently performs a multitude of services within SOF, e.g., training, organizational consultation, research, and the prevention and treatment of stress reactions, but all of the current positions have as their basis the assessment and selection of soldiers for critical tasks."[9]

Current Selection Process

Criteria for recruitment and selection into SOF and CIA today are similar to those used by OSS, although with a more extensive evaluation process. Today every SOF component has its own selection process that is rigorous and looks for very specific qualities. Psychological assessment, introduced by OSS as a tool to screen prospective recruits, continues to be a key component of today's selection process for entry into Army SF, the Ranger Regiment, SEALs, the Air Force Special Operations Combat

---

[6] Donald W. MacKinnon, *How assessment centers were started in the United States: The OSS Assessment Program* (Pittsburgh, PA: Development Dimensions International, 1974, 1980).
[7] Louie M. Banks, ―The History of Special Operations Psychological Selection."
[8] Charles M. Simpson III, *Inside the Green Berets: The First Thirty Years - A History of the U.S. Army Special Forces* (Novato CA: Presidio Press, 1983).
[9] Louie M. Banks, ―The History of Special Operations Psychological Selection."

Advisory Aviation unit, and is used by CIA to identify candidates for its clandestine service. In most cases candidates are assessed for mental, physical, and psychological qualities as well as their ability to work in a small team. The competitive selection process, coupled with technological training and education, produces a SOF operator who is adaptable, culturally aware, innovative, mature, self-assured, and self-reliant.[10]

Today SF recruiters look for many of the same attributes and qualities that the OSS did, but the process has become much more refined over the years. A downside of the refined process is that it comes with specific requirements for output, so the selection process can be manipulated to meet number requirements which results in reduced quality and violates a SOF truth that quality is more important than quantity. In addition, another complaint includes the concept of cloning, in which the majority of SF operators seem to display the same physical characteristics and are homogeneous, described more directly, they are mostly all ―athletic-looking white guys.‖[11] ―Many parts of the SOF community are very white and conservative,‖ according to a recent Washington Times article on the repeal of Don‗t Ask Don‗t Tell.[12] The article also cites a Rand study that stated in 1999 that ―blacks are particularly underrepresented [in SOF] when compared with their presence in the source populations.‖[13]

Selection into and participation in the Special Forces Qualification Course, also referred to as the ―Q Course‖ begins with an assessment: a battery of psychological and experiential tests and exercises, named Special Forces Assessment and Selection (SFAS). They address social as well as physical abilities. SFAS, a three-week precursor course held at a training facility near Fort Bragg, is ―designed to see if a soldier has what it takes to serve‖ on an Operational Detachment A–team (ODA), and is designed to assess a soldier‗s intellectual and physical aptitude for successful completion of Special Forces training and suitability to serve as positive contributing member of the Special Forces Regiment. The assessment of a soldier attending SFAS is based on the SF core attributes: integrity, courage, perseverance, personal responsibility, professionalism, adaptability, and team player (team work) capability. The average selection rate is 40 percent.[14]

---

[10] Jessica Glicken Turnley, *Cross-Cultural Competence and Small Groups: Why SOF are the way SOF are,* JSOU Report 11-1 (Tampa, FL: JSOU Press, March 2011).

[11] This quote was repeated by several current and former SOF operators during this study.

[12] Rowan Scarborough, ―Special Forces Wary Of 'Don't Ask' Repeal,‖ *The Washington Times* (28 December, 2010), p.1.

[13] Margaret C. Harrell, et. al., *Barriers to Minority Participation in Special Operations Forces* (Santa Monica, CA: Rand Corporation, 1999).

[14] ―Special Forces - Shooters and Thinkers,‖ U.S. Army, http://www.army.mil/article/29315/ Special_Forces ___Shooters_and _thinkers/, accessed December 2010.

Each SF candidate is screened as soon as he arrives through a battery of psychological tests, and his performance is evaluated throughout the Q Course. The Minnesota Multi-phasic Personality Inventory (MMPI, now the MMPI-2) is used to identify candidates with abnormal personality symptoms and disorders. The General Ability Measure for Adults (GAMA) is used to measure non-verbal intelligence and aptitude. The Test of Adult Basic Education (TABE) is used to measure basic academic achievement. Intelligence and problem solving aptitude are also measured with the Wonderlic Personnel Test. Soldiers with abnormal psychopathology, a history of poor performance, or are considered a high risk are personally evaluated by a psychologist. The candidate's ―trainability (intelligence) and suitability (psychopathology)‖ to complete training and ultimately perform the duties of an SF operator are evaluated. Candidates who demonstrate a consistent lack of cognitive and reasoning ability throughout these tests and or display severe abnormal psychopathology are dropped from selection. Similar to the OSS evaluation program, SF candidates are also put through a series of grueling physical and mental tasks designed to measure their character, commitment, and application of acumen under pressure. Candidates are presented challenges and their identified task performance is carefully observed and evaluated in both individual and in grouped settings. Candidates must meet minimum physical standards measured using the Army Physical Fitness Test (APFT) as well as a series of physical endurance events.[15] At any time throughout the assessment the candidate can voluntarily withdraw.

Upon completion of the SF assessment program, a selection board comprised of USAJFKSWCS senior leadership is convened to review the performance of each candidate presented to determine their trainability and suitability. Only candidates who displayed shortcomings in one or more area of assessment are considered by the board. The board evaluates each individual presented as a ―whole man‖ to include a background and service history of each questionable candidate. The board votes, and the board president provides the tie-breaker vote if required. It is important to note that this process is used to identify unsuitable individuals and is not necessarily used to screen successful candidates. Getting ―selected‖ at SFAS is the assessment phase (Phase 1) before being allowed to continue onto the following phases of the Q Course. A candidate must still complete the next four phases of training to graduate as a Special Forces qualified Soldier and be assigned to an Operational Detachment A, properly known as an A-Team.[16]

---

[15] L. M. Banks, ―The History of Special Operations Psychological Selection.‖
[16] Ibid.

The 75th Ranger Regiment is the U.S. Army's premier light infantry unit. Partially based on the success of the SF assessment process, a psychological assessment or Ranger Assessment and Selection Program (RASP) was added to an already arduous Army Ranger selection process. The RASP has similar technical characteristics to the SFAS.[17]

The Navy has also advanced its recruiting and assessment of candidates to serve as SEAL operators under the Naval Special Warfare Command. Until recently, the Navy SEAL recruitment process focused solely on assessing the physical fitness of potential candidates. Candidates either passed or failed the Physical Screening Test (PST) as a prerequisite to formal assessment into the elite force. Quoted in a recent article in USA Today, "the ideal candidate is an athlete in his early to mid-20s, plays water polo or competes in triathlons." Once identified some SEAL candidates are personally assigned a mentor and prepare up to a year before beginning Basic Underwater Demolition/SEAL (BUD/S), the Navy's formal SEAL qualification course. In 2010 the Navy graduated a record 277 from BUD/S.[18]

In 2008 the Navy added the Computerized Special Operations Resilience Test (C-SORT) to the PST as another discriminator to determine readiness to attend BUD/S. C-SORT is a psychological test that screens for characteristics such as a candidate's ability to function as a team player, to be motivated to withstand pain, and his ability to focus on an end goal while dealing with the immediate situations.[19]

The 160th Special Operations Aviation Regiment (SOAR)[20] known as the "Night Stalkers" is the Army's elite aviation regiment providing dedicated rotary-wing, special operations aviation support to the Joint SOF community. In the early years of the unit's existence it suffered from a very high accident rate during training, which also resulted in a high number of casualties. In addition to an assessment of technical flying capabilities all SOAR candidates were later evaluated with a formal psychological assessment. This assessment process has also recently been expanded to assess its newly assigned support personnel.[21]

---

[17] Ibid.

[18] Thomas Vanden Brook, "U.S. Special Ops Forces Vital in Afghan War," *USA TODAY*, (December 27, 2010).

[19] Discussion with Dr. Kristen E. Horgen, research scientist involved with developing the C-SORT, December 2010.

[20] In 2011 the Army Special Operations Aviation Command (ARSOAC) was established underneath U.S. Army Special Operations Command. The 160th SOAR is assigned to ARSOAC.

[21] Mathew N. Butler, "A Few Good Men: Support Soldier Selection and Training," *Special Warfare Magazine* Vol. 23, Issue 6 (Nov-Dec 2010).

Combat Aviation Advisory (CAA) operators from the 6th Special Operations Squadron (SOS) are U.S. Air Force SOF advisors ̶ specifically trained and tasked to assess, train, advise and assist foreign aviation forces in airpower employment, sustainment, and force integration." CAA candidates are screened and selected through a formal process before beginning the Combat Aviation Advisor Mission Qualification Course (CAAMQ), a challenging program ̶ intended to produce foreign language proficient, regionally-oriented, politically astute and culturally aware aviation advisory experts."[22]

CIA Selection and Recruitment: An OSS Tradition

To meet its initial demands for experts and others with advanced knowledge of world affairs and culture, Donovan and the OSS recruited heavily from Ivy League universities, industry and technology organizations, and socialites. In general, the current CIA recruitment and operational selection process is similar to the OSS model, but it has changed in parallel with the organizational growth and expansion of CIA's current mission.[23] Like its OSS predecessor, CIA also relied upon the Ivy League as a prospective talent pool for recruitment, and the organization still recruits significantly from Ivy League schools as well as other universities across the country.

Like the OSS and unlike most government organizations, CIA still has a pick of employees and is still attracting the best that America has to offer because of mystique and patriotism. The CIA Recruitment Center coordinates recruitment initiatives and monitors hiring needs and metrics to meet CIA mission requirements. According to the CIA careers web site,[24] ̶ the Recruitment Center aims to:

- Recruit and hire the most highly qualified and diverse men and women to ensure a workforce with a broad range of ethnic and cultural backgrounds, language expertise, and educational experiences
- Establish and foster productive partnerships nationwide with colleges, universities, professional networks, and organizations that are key sources of top talent
- Interact with minority affinity groups to establish long-term relationships and strategies for recruiting candidates
- Reach a nationwide audience of competitive candidates for career opportunities through innovative advertising and marketing"

---

[22] Combat Aviation Advisor Factsheet, US Air Force, 2011, available at http://www.af.mil/information/factsheets/factsheet.asp?id=18763, accessed December 2010.

[23] Rob Townley, Conversation with OSS historian and descendant of OSS veteran, November 2010.

[24] Careers, CIA, available at https://www.cia.gov/careers/index.html, accessed December 2010.

CIA recruiters canvas the country visiting college campuses, professional conferences, and putting on job fairs searching for suitable candidates with specialized knowledge and skills that can be used across the organization. Thousands of patriotic candidates also apply through the public web site and submit resumes by mail or through current employees. This is the front-door Human Resources system, and then there are all the other ways, including recruitment of former military personnel, many with special operations background. According to a recent estimate, there are some 1000 candidates for each available opportunity.

What were the criteria for selection of the OSS and how does it compare to the Question 1?

Selection for OSS was much less in-depth when compared to today. OSS recruited Americans from all ranks and strata, but concentrated on those already with some military experience to reduce the amount of basic military training required. General Donovan surrounded himself with top administrative men, and he believed qualified soldiers with language skills and cultural backgrounds to operate overseas could be found among ethnic groups (first- or second-generation Americans) in the U.S. He directed his recruiters to search for men who were ―calculatingly reckless with disciplined daring, who are trained for aggressive action."[25] It has been said that Donovan would refuse no one who wanted to go overseas and do something worthwhile even if they did not fit the regulations.[26]

―Donovan recruited Americans who, like himself, traveled abroad or studied world affairs and, in that age, such people often represented ‗the best and the brightest' at East Coast (Ivy League) universities, businesses, and law firms."[27] According to some historical accounts, General Donovan told candidates to ―write me a memorandum saying how you could be of service to this organization, and if I agree with you, you're hired." Volunteers responded to advertisements looking for persons with foreign language capabilities and who would be interested in special assignments.[28] Following an interview to determine general suitability, they reported to Washington D.C. for paramilitary

---

[25] William J. Morgan, *The OSS and I* (New York, NY: W.W. Norton and Company, 1957).

[26] Stewart Alsop and Thomas Braden, *Sub Rosa: The OSS and American Espionage* (New York, NY: Reynal and Hitchcock, 1964).

[27] The Office of Strategic Services: The Forerunner of Today's CIA, 2008, available at https://www.cia.gov/news-information/featured-story-archive/2008-featured-story-archive/office-of strategic-services.html, accessed December 2010.

[28] Aron Bank, *From OSS to Green Berets* (Novato, CA: Presidio Press, 1986).

training. Those selected for overseas deployment would then undergo additional, more intense training in England.

The world has moved on since the 1940s and 1950s, and the student bodies of today's Ivy League are nearly night and day from that of the first quarter of the 20th century, statistically speaking.[29] Today, if one goes into the Harvard bookstore, among the racks and racks of clothing emblazoned with crimson and white you'll find that the rack of athletic-fit t-shirts with _Harvard Business School' (HBS) written across the chest is always full—even for less than $10, the store can hardly sell one. This small indicator begs the same question that Donovan is reported to have asked of his recruiters, ―Where are the PhDs, who can win a bar-fight?‖[30]

As a Master's program, HBS is a school now accessible to many in the corporate world through their offering of truncated executive MBA programs and the like, and the student body in general is far more of an amalgam of both American society and the international business community than it once was. According to one estimate, approximately 70 percent of the most recent executive MBA program class were not American citizens.[31]

These circumstances have not always been the case. During the first half of the 20th century, for example, the Ivy League was, by no small margin, a _finishing school' for the children of the U.S. and international diplomatic communities. The children of ambassadors and consular officers who grew up in Europe, Latin America, and Eurasia in the 1920s, were raised speaking at least one language other than English, and attended European universities for their undergraduate degrees, followed their parents back to the U.S. for their _twilight tours' with the foreign service where many of the children attended Ivy League schools for their graduate degree. This made the Ivy League the most accessible location with the highest concentration of educated U.S. citizens with practical (not school taught) foreign language proficiency who had _ready made' social and political networks in Europe. By the time OSS recruiters or Donovan's own network identified them, all they needed was a short stint of paramilitary training to teach them how to harness their networks in Europe in support of the war effort, which an overwhelming number of them did as Jedburghs or Operations Group (OG) officers.[32]

---

[29] Rob Townley, 2010.

[30] Although this quote is commonly accepted and widely attributed to Donovan, its origin cannot be confirmed.

[31] Rob Townley, 2010.

[32] Ibid.

The makeup of student bodies in the Ivy League has changed dramatically, and likewise the CIA's focus in recruiting from such schools has changed. The latter change in focus is a function of two primary circumstances: the growth of the original OSS network within the higher end of the U.S. academic community, and the expansion of CIA's roles in intelligence collection and analysis. In the postwar years, many of OSS's recruits from the Ivy League either returned to their posts in academia or stayed on to become part of CIA. These officers' wartime experience had a cascading effect on the recruitment pools available to CIA in the following decades, as professors or graduate students with OSS backgrounds moved on to other academic institutions and gained access to new pools of prospective candidates. In this way, the CIA's recruitment efforts have since gained purchase across a broad spectrum of the U.S. academic community, riding on the coattails of the social and career progressions of Donovan's original recruits. In some fashion, this circumstance lends credence to OSS's _Oh So Social' moniker, which, while it was often used to deride the service's organizational character, in fact hits on some of the very reasons OSS was effective; many times the deciding factor in the success both in the conduct of intelligence and unconventional warfare is _who' you know, not _what' you know.[33]

Was there a set of criteria in the selection process to determine grade level of appointment? Was there a set of criteria in the selection process to determine job specialty and assignment location? CONUS or OCONUS? Is there any evidence that this was an effective system?

There was no formal assessment process to enter the OSS in its first year. According to Dr. Donald MacKinnon, a psychologist who pioneered assessment and selection programs for both the OSS and CIA, personnel entered the OSS through the following:

- recruitment of military personnel by the Personnel Procurement Branch (PPB)
- recruitment of civilians by the Civilian Personnel Branch (CPB)
- recruitment of both military and civilian personnel through the initiative of individual OSS members[34]

As stated earlier, by the middle of 1943 reports from the field indicated that there were issues with some deployed personnel.[35] According to MacKinnon, ―nobody knew

---

[33] Ibid.

[34] Donald W. MacKinnon, ―How assessment centers were started in the United States: The OSS Assessment Program," *Studies In Intelligence*, 23, No. 3 (Fall 1979), available at http://www.ddiworld.com/DDIWorld/media/whitepapers/HowAssessmentCentersWereStarted_mg_ddi.pdf ?ext=.pdf, accessed December 2010.

[35] L. M. Banks, ―The History of Special Operations Psychological Selection."

who would make a good spy or an effective guerrilla fighter. Consequently, large numbers of misfits were recruited from the very beginning, and this might have continued had it not been for several disastrous operations such as one in Italy for which, on the assumption that it takes dirty men to do dirty works, some OSS men were recruited directly from the ranks of Murder, Inc. and the Philadelphia Purple Gang."[36]

OSS Psychological Assessment Program

The OSS Assessment Program encountered other shortcomings due to the haste in which it was established.[37] According to MacKinnon ―psychological assessment staff lacked knowledge about the assignments, most of them novel, to which new recruits would be sent. Without job analyses, the psychologists did not know specifically for what they were assessing. Operations experts were needed to write job descriptions, but initially there were none in the field. At best, job assignments were described by single terms: language expert, cartographer, news analyst… Only those destined for overseas assignment were assessed; those who remained in the United States were exempt."[38]

Special Forces "Whole Man" Assessment

The ―whole man" assessment approach used by Special Forces psychologists to evaluate a soldier's suitability to become an SF operator is based loosely on the practice used by OSS and is used also by CIA to select candidates to undergo training as operations officers.[39] The ―whole man" assessment model initiated by the OSS was applied in part because the civilian psychologists assigned to the OSS assessment program did not know what specific tasks and skills where required in the field. MacKinnon wrote:

> In the beginning, the lack of specific knowledge led us to conclude that assessments could not be made of the specific skills of a given candidate for a specific job but rather in each case, an assessment of the ‗man as a whole,' should be made, including the general structure of his being, and his strengths and weaknesses for rather generally described environments and situations.[40]

---

[36] Donald W. MacKinnon, ―How assessment centers were started in the United States: The OSS Assessment Program," *Studies In Intelligence*, 23, No. 3 (Fall 1979).

[37] Ibid.

[38] Ibid.

[39] Louie M. Banks, *The Office of Strategic Services Psychological Selection Program* (Fort Leavenworth, KS: 1995)

[40] Donald W. MacKinnon, ―How assessment centers were started in the United States: The OSS Assessment Program, 1979.

This led to a discovery that very few recruits were actually assigned to the billet they were recruited for. People would be hired and show up in Washington only to be asked ―Do you have any idea what OSS might have hired you for?"[41] In other cases they hired two people for the same job, such as the case where two people were hired to head the Research Section of the Division of Special Information, so one was given the title ―Director" and the other ―Chief." The lack of a specific system meant that there were men who did daring missions with strategic implications and those who spent their service doing nothing but travelling the world on a high priority at government expense. The only thing that appeared to impact assignment location was language capability and cultural familiarity. It was not relevant that the OSS tried to fit the right person to a position. Training including paramilitary operations lasted up to eight months after selection and in some instances the initial assignment would change as the needs of the war advanced.[42]

In addition to establishing the psychological assessment program discussed above, the OSS defined its human resource pool and selected personnel on the basis of three primary sets of holistic attributes as they pertained to each service member or employee: specific discipline or skill, ethnic or geographic background (access, experience), and general temperament (personality). The apparent overlap, or lack thereof, with regard to discipline and background was often a deciding factor in the selection of an individual for service with the OSS, and furthermore informed the type and character of the assignment for which the individual evaluated would be chosen. Though this system manifested in a number of different forms (PPB activities, spot assessment, referral, etc), it is important to note that the selection process was not predicated primarily upon the evaluation of basic human predispositions or physical abilities, but on the identification and evaluation of practical knowledge, experience, and access that the individual might provide in support of OSS‗s requirements. To this end, the OSS made a point of seeking out individuals with existing skill sets that the military did not or could not develop organically that might be of use in military or intelligence applications.

The above assertion is borne out in a number of larger OSS or COI recruitment efforts, but is most readily apparent in two cases: the selection of ‗Donovan‗s 300,‗ and

---

[41] Richard Harris Smith, *OSS: The Secret History of America's First Central Intelligence Agency* (Berkeley, CA: University of California Press; First Lyons Press, paperback edition, 1972).
[42] Donald W. MacKinnon, ―How assessment centers were started in the United States: The OSS Assessment Program, 1979.

the immediate consequences of Donovan's relationship with the British as illustrated in correspondence in 1941 between him and Commander Ian Fleming.[43]

First, consider the relationship General Donovan as Coordinator of Information (COI) had with _the 300.' During the years between WWI and WWII, Donovan, a prominent Wall Street lawyer, travelled extensively throughout Europe as either a private citizen or at the behest of President Roosevelt. During this period he observed the rise of the Nazi Party in Germany, and particularly the Reichstag's renewal of the _Enabling Act' in 1937, which set in motion a number of social and political changes in Europe that led Donovan to conclude that war was inevitable. In the interest of maintaining as much knowledge as possible regarding the irredentist rhetoric of Nazi party leadership, Donovan developed a network of largely academic contacts in both Europe and the U.S. who were either expatriates or citizens of nations that bordered Germany.

After he was appointed to the post of COI in summer 1941, Donovan reactivated many of these contacts and gathered a number of additional ones to aid him in producing a complete picture of both the German population and leadership as well as that of those countries immediately surrounding Germany in an effort to understand Nazi intentions and put the Nazi leadership's activities in context. Donovan placed a number of these contacts, estimated at approximately 300, on retainer for the COI as the organization developed a foundation of knowledge to advise the Roosevelt administration. Many of these individuals were selected not because of their technical knowledge of the German military, but because of their proven practical experience or knowledge of the political, cultural, economic, environmental, linguistic or other concerns of anthropological or behavioral nature in Europe. As such, their contributions to the COI's planning efforts produced what could be characterized as a predecessor to a current day _national intelligence estimate' that was almost wholly focused on the populations of Europe rather than the governments, and on the societal, rather than technological, aspects of European nations and international discourse.

Something to be considered when examining the COI's recruitment and use of such individuals is the _lead time' involved given the timeline and nature of what was to become the multi-theater conflict of WWII. Donovan began developing a knowledge base (and in some respects what could be considered a capability development roadmap) on conditions in Europe years prior to America's entry into the war. This knowledge base offered the OSS a significant depth of operational context and currency in many critical aspects of its development. By the time the U.S. began moving toward the commitment

---

[43] Rob Townley, 2010.

of more than materiel support to the British war effort, Donovan already had an informational advantage over his more conventional counterparts in the armed services given their comparative poverty of knowledge on many subjects germane to the analysis of the German military industrial base that was, at the time, supporting the blitzkrieg, and which would later become the large focus of the Allied bombing campaign in Europe.

By the time the OSS was activated, Donovan already knew the general mix of manpower and skills that would be required to carry out his mission, and was able to deploy trained, informed, and effective teams into combat alongside the British Special Operations Executive (SOE) well in advance of any other American military ground force. Without first developing the capability to maintain a measure of historical perspective and mid-term currency in operational context regarding the European theater of operations, the OSS may not have recruited the right sort of personnel to meet the intellectual, as well as the physical, demands of an incredibly dynamic operational environment.

The original recruitment and use of _the 300' also helped to create another, equally important part of the OSS's foundation: the process helped to found the service with a reverence and reliance on the history of the populations in which it was to operate. This reliance, in operational terms, translated culturally into one of the more deceptive traits of the OSS. Though each OSS team (Jedburghs, OGs, Secret Intelligence detachments, etc.) made what would be considered _small moves' on the battlefield when considered independently, each small move was purposely designed to take advantage of existing circumstance in order to produce disproportionate result, or to compliment other _small moves' in order to build the critical mass necessary to achieve a large goal. At its core, this characteristic may be superficially compared to the adage _think globally, act locally.'

OSS leadership did not need to micromanage operations in the field to coordinate these kinds of activities; rather, they occurred naturally. To consider in linear fashion how this was possible given the relatively limited communications infrastructure of the period, OSS personnel assigned to combat or intelligence collection duties overseas were selected by men whose knowledge of their enemy was steeped in a holistic understanding of their proposed operating environment.

As such, the selection teams were predisposed to choose men with a similar rich understanding, paired with specific skill sets as necessary. Once in the field, OSS officers did not need to communicate with each other or their headquarters constantly or over long distances to achieve operational unity – their common perspective and near native familiarity with their operating environment produced this unity of action naturally, such that each _small move' intrinsically complemented another. When considered in the aggregate, OSS operations in Europe during WWII resembled less something regulated by command and signal, and more something governed by common strategic purpose and well-heeled instinct.

Donovan's close collaboration with the British leading up to the beginning of WWII provided a second and readily apparent influence on the OSS's recruitment activities. During Donovan's assignments on behalf of President Roosevelt as a special liaison to Whitehall, Donovan gained much insight (whether arranged or objective) into the logic behind the SOE and Special Intelligence Service (SIS) operations in Europe. In later correspondence with his colleague Fleming during the summer of 1941, Donovan asked him how he should initially devise the makeup of his headquarters staff. Fleming's response was somewhat flippant, but confirmed many of Donovan's earlier assertions on the nature and requirements for the prosecution of successful guerrilla warfare. Fleming recommended that Donovan locate and enlist the services of a number of reputable professionals from American industry or society to serve as senior officers or department heads.

The logic behind Fleming's recommendation for recruitment was twofold: first, the proven track record of these individuals obviously indicated that each would be an asset to the OSS from a simple managerial standpoint. However, the more important aspect of these recommendations was that the recruitment of these individuals represented a harnessing of the _best of breed' from the U.S. as a nation, and with that came expertise, access and resources associated with the industrial or societal sector in which each individual had distinguished himself. By adding these individuals to the ranks, the OSS gained the ability to leverage large parts of American society in support of the war effort. Again, these recruitments were small moves, but they had disproportionate effects when considered in context of America's trajectory into the war. Several of these recruitments, such as the relationship that the OSS developed with Henry Luce (influential publisher and creator of the Time/Life magazine empire), long outlasted the OSS's existence, and became valuable assets to our nation's national security apparatus both during and after WWII. However, it can be conjectured that it was not the distinguished individual, but the network in which he existed, that represented value to the OSS as an organization.

What are your recommendations for the selection process for special operations warriors in the 21st century?

The most important thing in selection is to remember that quality (suitability) is more important than quantity (numbers) and that SOF cannot be mass produced. Our selection processes are sound as long as they are followed.

S1: There needs to be a selection process for non-operator service-provided capability personnel (enablers). We spend an enormous amount of effort and money to select the right operator but other than a few exceptions do nothing to screen the individuals who will be supporting the operator. These support personnel are absolutely critical to mission success, and yet SOF generally accepts whoever the service provides. The challenge to selecting support personnel is that the services may not provide enough candidates to allow a rigorous selection, but there should be some system to evaluate a support person's potential for serving in a SOF unit.

S2: Target recruitment efforts in ethnic neighborhoods and enclaves in the United States where immigrants from around the world settled. Middle Eastern and South Asian immigrant communities can be found in the following areas:

- Arabian Village, Detroit and Dearborn, Michigan
- Assyrian District, northern Chicago, Illinois
- Chaldean Town, Detroit, Michigan
- East Dearborn, Michigan (Iraqi)
- Little Arabia, Albany Park, Chicago, Illinois
- Little Arabia Anaheim (Orange County), Anaheim, California
- Little Kabul, Fremont, California (the largest Afghan population in the United States in 2001)
- Little Persia, Los Angeles, California (Iranian)
- South Paterson/Little Ramallah, Paterson, New Jersey and Clifton, New Jersey
- Little Tel Aviv, Miami, Florida[44]

Similar ethnic enclaves with immigrants who speak various African dialects, Asian languages, or Spanish exist in many other areas of the U.S., such as numerous cities with a China Town, a Little Havana, or a Little Somalia. Many immigrants are eager to prove their patriotism and loyalty to their new nation and simply need to be asked to join the military.

S3: Cultural awareness: To promote development of cultural awareness and advanced language skills, a quote was extracted from a November 2010 statement made by John R. Clapper, the Director Of National Intelligence: ―we need to build and maintain a workforce that represents the rich diversity of the world we live in: a work force that reflects different cultural backgrounds, ethnicities and heritage, languages, races, gender, orientation, abilities, and ideas."[45] Despite previous efforts that have not

---

[44] List of Ethnic Enclaves in North America, Wikipedia, (n.d.), available at http://en.wikipedia.org/wiki/List_of_named_ethnic_enclaves_in_North_American_cities, accessed December 2010.
[45] John R. Clapper, ―Statement on Intelligence Community Equal Opportunity and Diversity," Director of National Intelligence, signed 10 November 2010.

been as successful or effective as we would like, we should continue to look for methods to deliberately recruit people with the desired language and cultural background.

S4: Finally, in terms of selection process, focus on recruiting or getting the word out to current service members or those who are considering joining the services that may potentially qualify as a special operations warrior. Extend the search across service organizations to identify current service members, irrespective of service, who may possess special skills of interest to SOF. Expand the recruiting effort by using current and former SOF operators to recruit in high schools, junior and four-year colleges and universities to better inform potential candidates about the positive and negative aspects of SOF. In a manner similar to OSS, selecting candidates based on already acquired skill sets (e.g., free fall sky diving, SCUBA, use of compass and orienteering, language, cultural, computers, etc.) may be of value. Focus recruitment efforts on those who have been successful in the scouting movement because many of them, particularly if they have achieved the Eagle or Explorer rank, will have mastered some of the above skills being sought. Even with such a good head start, of course the difficulty lies in the actual training required to make a candidate SOF-qualified. Targeted recruiting efforts, however, for potential candidates, who already possess a specific required skill set rather than the current recruiting for generalist candidates, should result in identifying motivated candidates ready to undergo the rigor of SOF training.

S5: One recent hurdle to recruiting has been the inability to obtain clearances for new immigrants to the U.S., and is a significant issue in the current environment where SOF operators routinely work with classified information. The Lodge-Philbin Act better known as the Lodge Act was passed in 1950 and was in effect through 1959. It allowed foreign nationals to serve in the U.S. Armed forces with the ultimate reward of US residency and citizenship. Former OSS members and new Army SF soldiers were common beneficiaries of the policy.[46] Recommend taking another look at introducing a new law similar to the Lodge Act to encourage the recruitment of foreign nationals or other recent immigrants seeking U.S. citizenship through military service.

S6: ―USSOCOM does not normally have operational authority over deployed forces, the plans and operations themselves are executed by the Geographic Combatant Commanders.‖[47] Similarly, USSOCOM will require the support from the other military services to implement major improvements to its recruitment and selection process. Recommend that the USSOCOM J-1 (Personnel) be granted authority to manage all

---

[46] L. Morgan Banks, ―The History of Special Operations Psychological Selection.‖
[47] Extracted from Admiral Eric Olson's testimony to the Senate Armed Service Committee as USSOCOM commander, June 2009.

personnel issues, including recruitment and selection, related to the entire force and not just limited to the command level as is the current situation. This will allow the J-1 to have visibility throughout SOF and to be able to monitor and respond to recruitment needs across the force as well as better coordinate force-wide requests for support from the other military services.

S7: Special Operations warriors, like OSS agents of the past, need to be of a certain mind, body, and motivation type. In terms of ―mind,‖ recommend SOF evaluators make even greater use of the assessment process by having candidates complete a battery of psychological and aptitude assessments to determine a host of specific characteristics required for success in today‘s SOF. Assuming the selection committee knows what characteristics are determined desirable they can add this to their consideration. Both body and motivation type are covered in the selection and training process current candidates undergo.

S8: Build a 360-degree feedback mechanism into the assessment process to add to its effectiveness of measuring the whole man. In this 360-degree feedback assessment the candidate‘s immediate supervisor(s), colleagues, and subordinates would receive an on-line feedback assessment for each of the identified raters. The 360-degree feedback assessment gives a more complete view of the candidate in terms of multiple perspectives.

Are there new authorities required to achieve the recommendations?
New authorities, such as a new Lodge Act, would be required to recruit non-citizens into the military. The U.S. military services already have the authority to recruit and offer direct commissions to medical and legal specialists. Another program, The MAVNI is an extended pilot program, under the authorization of the Department of Defense. It allows the services ―to recruit certain legal aliens whose skills are considered to be vital to the national interest‖[48] such as medical professionals (nurses, doctors) and enlisted individuals with ―special language and cultural backgrounds… those in certain nonimmigrant visa categories can obtain citizenship without first becoming a permanent resident.‖ Background security investigations, required for security clearances are currently an issue being addressed by USSOCOM; foreign nationals from certain focus countries are having trouble obtaining the appropriate level of clearance to be of use to SOF.[49]

---

[48] Military Accessions Vital to the National Interest (MAVNI) Factsheet, available at http://www.defense.gov/news/mavni-fact-sheet.pdf, accessed December 2010.
[49] Input provided by the USSOCOM J1 (personnel) representatives contributing to the OSS study.

Similar to the Lodge Act, Section 329 of the Immigration and Nationality Act (INA), also known as ―wartime naturalization" allows service members ―who serve during specifically designated periods of hostilities" to achieve citizenship without having to first apply for permanent residency.[50] The MAVNI program derives its authority from this section of the INA. Extension of the MAVNI program was a priority for Admiral Olson and USSOCOM as he also included an endorsement of the program in his September 2009 Posture Statement.[51]

Will there be new levels of resourcing required (not numbers of dollars rather a description of resources-education, equipment...)?

An expanded recruitment and selection effort probably would require additional resources, recruiters and screeners, and training staff for processing them into their respective SOF organizations. Moreover, the influx of additional personnel, especially if they require the granting of a security clearance, would also require additional security and other investigative personnel to process the requests for clearances. In the case of immigrants wanting to join the military, part of the problem with clearances is that investigators cannot look into a person's background overseas prior to their arrival in the U.S. To successfully recruit immigrant personnel, USSOCOM might require its own investigative branch to research an applicant's background overseas. It would also require additional training courses to prepare the applicant for existing training courses, much like was run in the 18X program, an enlistment option which provides soldiers an opportunity to ―try out" for Special Forces.

Selecting support personnel would also require additional recruiters and an organizational structure to conduct the selection. It could be minimal, as a useful selection for support personnel could be as simple as an application, a review of the applicant's records, and an interview. The question would be whether SOF can select enough support personnel to fill the required billets.

---

[50] Naturalization Process for the Military (n.d.), U.S. Citizen and Immigration Services website, available at http://www.uscis.gov/portal/site/uscis/menuitem.5af9bb95919f35e66f614176543f6d1a/?vgnextoid=858921 e54dc3f110VgnVCM1000004718190aRCRD&vgnextchannel=8a2f6d26d17df110VgnVCM100000471819 0aRCRD, accessed December 2010.
[51] Admiral Olson reiterated his continued support for the MAVNI program in his March 2011 Posture Statement.

Organization

This section summarizes the approach the OSS took toward the organization, the current organizations of U.S. Army Special Forces and CIA, and offers some recommendations for application as it relates to U.S. Special Operations Forces (USSOF). Judgments expressed are drawn from reading OSS-related literature, discussions with military officers and civilian leaders from the office of the Deputy Assistant Secretary of Defense for Special Operations and Counterterrorism (DASD/SO/CT), USAJFKSWCS, USASOC, and current and former officers at CIA. Research was organized according to a set of Study Questions which were developed to guide and trigger discussion during the seminar and yield concrete recommendations.

Study Questions on Organization

How was the OSS structured during the war (Jedburghs and Operational Groups)? Was this an effective structure?

The OSS was, according to legendary CIA historian and analyst Thomas F. Troy, –a novel attempt in American history to organize research, intelligence, propaganda, subversion, and commando operations as a unified and essential feature of modern warfare; a _Fourth Arm' of the military services."[52]

The organization of the OSS can be described as –purpose-built."[53] The structure was flexible enough to adjust itself to meet its objectives in support of the war effort. The organizational chart that follows for the OSS Organization can be a little deceptive to the casual reader. This chart was to satisfy the Washington, D.C. establishment sense of organization rather than the real functionality of it. The OSS was in reality a collection of small units supporting other small units within this organization. Each of these small units was mission-driven in defeating the enemy.

The reality of this chart was that almost everything was organized as small teams (small footprint). This was true from the Jedburghs (Jeds) to the Operational Groups[54] to the Board of Economic Warfare. The structure, with some exceptions, was functional in design and the exceptions, the Jeds and OGs, were more traditional military in their

---

[52] Thomas F. Troy, Donovan and the CIA: A History of the Establishment of the Central Intelligence Agency (Frederick, MD: University Publications of America, 1981).
[53] Rob Townley, discussions with JSOU Senior Fellows on the OSS, December 2010.
[54] Office of Strategic Services Field Manual No. 6, –Operational Group Field Manual - Strategic Services (Provisional)," 25 April 1944, declassified on March 12, 2009, National Archives Record Service (NARS).

respective design structure. These tactical units also had —bolt on" (additional function people or teams) personnel or teams that made them non-standard from their design. Under the Deputy Director of Strategic Services Operations were both Morale Operations (MO, propaganda) and the OGs. These units operated in the same areas, but with completely different missions. In spite of those operational differences they both had similar and therefore mutual objectives. They did mutually support each other within the AO, and at times it was synchronized to meet specific missions. OGs were regimental in design to fit their mission of recruiting, training, and commanding local guerrilla groups. MOs were organized by function and then by region.

By contrast, the Board of Economic Warfare and the Office of Economic Warfare Analysis (OEWA) were more complex. However, they still were —purpose-built" and maintained the small team approach. As an example, the Research and Analysis (R&A) section had only eight personnel to cover the entire effort in Europe.

The OSS began as a small organization by design. The OSS Organization Chart[55] is depicted below.

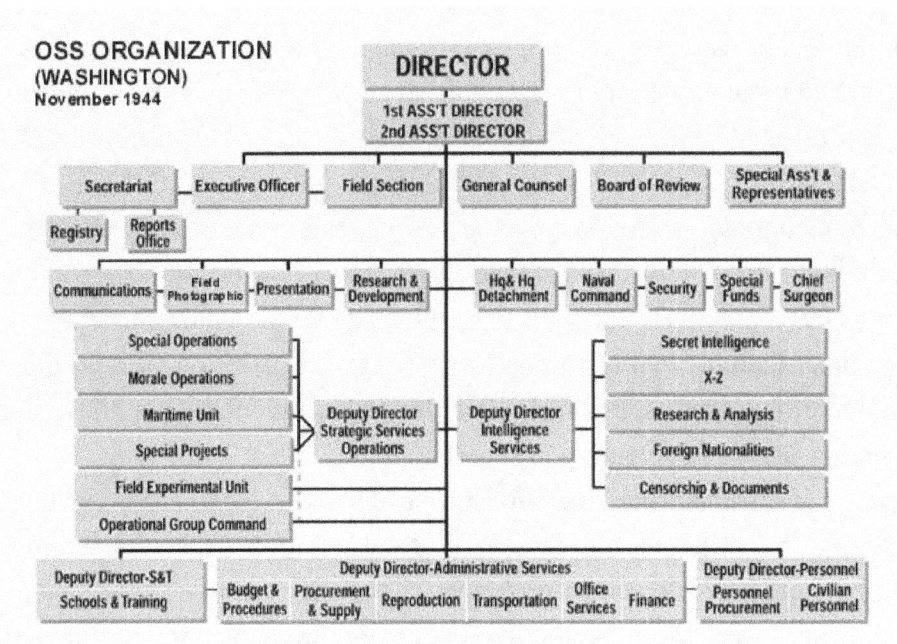

[55] Michael Warner, —What was OSS?" *The Office of Strategic Services: America's First Intelligence Agency* (e-book) 2007.

This organization was Major General Donovan's design based on his knowledge of business, Europe, and understanding of guerrilla warfare. He knew that his headquarters must remain small to be agile to apply its strategy from OSS Headquarters in Washington, D.C. to the units in the field. There was limited "two way" communications from his headquarters to the field units partly by design and partly because of the limitation of communication equipment. This did not mean that Donovan did not communicate or protect his commanders. Rather, he believed they were in the best position to make decisions, even ones that were not well received in their Theater of Operations. Donovan stood by his leaders' decisions, in many cases even if they were wrong.

Current Organization Construct

The answer to this question of structure has some obvious links from the OSS to USSOCOM/USASOC today and may lead to a path to the future of the SOF warrior. The most direct comparisons with the OSS are with Special Forces and to Military Information Support Operations (MISO) which were found under the Deputy Director for Strategic Services Operations. Special Operations (SO), Morale Operations (MO) and Operational Group Command are the links between the OSS and USASOC with SF and MISO.

Special Forces organizations take their heritage from the OSS in two areas. The Operational Groups, the first of these two areas, are roots for the SF Operational Detachment A. The two officers and 10 enlisted configuration is a spin-off from the OSS Operational Group structure of 34 men, including four officers and 30 enlisted. The basic structure of communications, demolitions, medics, and weapons specialties comes directly from the OSS. This OSS structure could be subdivided into two elements, with two officers and up to 15 enlisted in each team. Some of the officers and noncommissioned officers (NCOs) who set up the early Special Forces organizational framework came from either the OGs or the Jedburghs and sometimes both. Major General (retired) Jack Singlaub, Colonel (retired) Aaron Bank, and Major (retired) Caesar Civitella are three examples of that linkage.

The second area of the Special Forces mission concept of "by, through, and with" is derived from the OSS operational mission: "to organize, train and equip" local resistance groups to conduct guerrilla operations against their occupiers, as stated in the Operational

Groups Field Manual[56] for the OSS Special Operations units (Jedburghs and OGs). SF operates –by, through, and with" using Foreign Internal Defense (FID) or Unconventional Warfare (UW) techniques, and it still organizes, equips, and trains the locals. Direct Action certainly plays a role today as it did during WWII, but it was not the primary role then. The above mission tasks are part of USSOCOM's core activities and they have their roots in the OSS.

The use of Direct Action capability is also a direct link back to the OSS. This is one of the current SOF Core Activities, and it has become the signature of how the world sees Special Operations today. It may be causing the concern that the SF community is losing focus on the other Core Activities.[57] Consequently, many of the other SOF Core Activities are being challenged by the Conventional military by default and by over commitment to this single activity. Our assets are being stressed with repeat rotations to Iraq and Afghanistan at a very high percentage of our force structure.

Military Information Support Operations, formerly known as Psychological Operations (PSYOP), also has strong roots in the OSS under Morale Operations. As the COI, Donovan had control over all of the intelligence and information for the war effort to include propaganda. However, after Pearl Harbor, the President made a critical decision to separate –White" (overt, truthful, identifiable origins) and –Black" (covert, feel of truth, not clearly identifiable origins) propaganda, giving half (Black) to Donovan and half (White) to the Foreign Information Service (FIS) under Nelson Rockefeller. The FIS conducted radio broadcasts outside of military control with the expected clashes between conventional Services and Donovan's OSS. This remains true today; there is still separation between the types of psychological operations being conducted. Today, even on the military side of these types of operations are clashes over –turf" between Public Affairs (PAO), Information Operations (IO) and now MISO on issues of who does what and when at which target audience.

Morale Operations, established in January 1943, had two components: radio and printed materials. The components were intended to create havoc by the use of lies and deception to undermine enemy morale (military or population). The OSS did have trouble demonstrating the success of their operations, although there are cases where their deceptions were effective enough that they were picked up and reported by the allies as

---

[56] Office of Strategic Services Field Manual No. 6, *Operational Group Field Manual - Strategic Services (Provisional).*1944.
[57] Until 4 August 2011 the following were listed as SOF core activities: Foreign Internal Defense, Security Force Assistance, and Military Information Operations, See USSOCOM Factbook, 2010, p. 7.

true. Printed material included leaflets, false documents, false newspaper stories and death notices (rumors) to erode the enemy's will. By the end of World War II, there was sufficient enough belief in psychological warfare that the US military would include it in future warfare. This remains true today.

One common denominator between MISO and the OSS Morale Operations is language skills. Morale Operations required a high level, native-born, first hand knowledge of the particular language. This meant getting beyond the classroom and into the business/street-smart level of knowledge and cultural awareness. This was a reason the OSS got the —Oh, So Social"[58] negative reputation. Early recruits and leadership came from the part of American society that was educated overseas or was first generation US born. There were large numbers of Ivy League educated OSS warriors which contributed to this misunderstanding. Since the beginnings of SF, language skills and cross-cultural awareness have remained a constant challenge to the community. MISO has a greater challenge, because added to the language are some local cultural challenges.

MISO and Civil Affairs (CA) are being modified structurally and expanded in manpower. However, as two of the five SOF Truths state; —SOF cannot be mass produced"; Competent SOF cannot be created after emergencies occur". [59] Like SF soldiers, MISO and CA practitioners take time to develop and gain experience. Some of this experience is difficult to acquire by the military. For example, where do you find a CA guy on active duty who knows how to run a sewage plant?

The short answer for the OSS effectiveness depends on what theater and when the question was asked and by whom. Today, there is little doubt that both the CIA and Special Forces owe some varying degree of their existence and organization to the OSS. The most identifiable example is the SF A-team. The Afghan UW campaign in 2001 had its foundations built by the OSS in the 1940s.

What lessons were used from the OSS to create the CIA and SOF? Do those lessons still apply or has the structure of those organizations changed?
The short answer is that the selection process has had some minor changes, but the basic notions remain the same. Recruiters search for individuals with certain attributes that appear to be constant: physical fitness, intellect, self-control, outdoor skills, inter-personal skills, confident decision-making, and flexibility to adapt or adjust to most

---

[58] A.B. Kongrard, executive director of the CIA in his remarks to the Conference on the 60th Anniversary of the OSS in June 2002 put this well known accusation of the OSS into context that due to the war-driven haste in establishing the OSS Donovan relied on his network of elites to build the organization.
[59] USSOCOM Command Brief, November 2010.

situations. In short, Donavan tasked his recruiters with finding the PhD capable of winning the bar fight,[60] better still, capable of winning the fight the indirect way using ―by, through and with" the occupants of the bar.

Time and technology have, of course, caused some changes to occur already in the selection and recruitment of potential SOF warriors. The need for more technical skills and capability in cyber warfare are constantly being raised by the field, the theaters and by the public. Another technology that is also in high demand is the Unmanned Aerial Vehicles (UAV). This was not available during the OSS era, but Special Forces did have their own aviation assets. The following organizational chart illustrates the assignment of SOF dedicated aviation assets assigned to Special Forces Groups which had an aviation section[61] of fixed wing aircraft and included U-6 Beaver, U-10 Courier, and C-7A Caribou.[62]

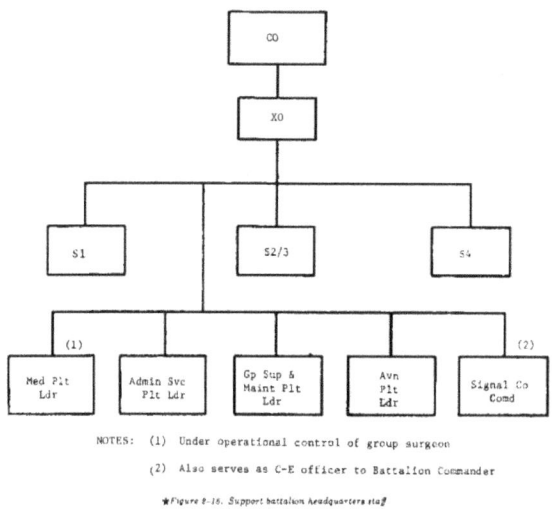

NOTES: (1) Under operational control of group surgeon

(2) Also serves as C-E officer to Battalion Commander

★Figure 8-16. Support battalion headquarters staff

One of the innovations that came out of early OSS requirements was parachute infiltration. During Vietnam, U.S. Army Special Forces developed the then new

---

[60] Walter Mess, quoted during the JSOU OSS-Society Seminar (video and transcript), 9 November 2009.

[61] Department of the Army Field Manual (FM) 31-21, ―US Army Special Forces Operations,"1969.

[62] Unit history of 134th Aviation Company Website. ―Unfortunately the Air Force never flew the Caribou like the Army. They were primarily interested in long-range ―throughput" missions while the Army used the Caribou for local support to remote Special Forces camps and similar missions. After the Air Force takeover, this incredible short field aircraft was phased out in favor of larger, high-speed conventional air transports. Consequently, the Special Forces and others were left without support. This was a role subsequently assumed by helicopter units." Available at http://unitpages military.com/unitpages/unit.do? id=892938, accessed December 2010.

technique of High Attitude Low Opening (HALO) insertion. This was developed by several Special Forces soldiers to include Master Sergeant (retired) Billy Waugh in October 1970.[63]

The two recent major engagements, Iraq and Afghanistan, should cause a need to revisit the role of women in SOF organizations to include Special Forces. If our grandmothers and mothers could be in the OSS to jump in and operate behind the lines (e.g. Virginia Hall[64] air-landed because she was missing a leg), why can't women be in operational units today? The Marines have women units attempting to interface directly with the women networks in Afghanistan. To be sure MISO and CA have long had women in their Table of Organizations and Equipment (TO&E). The question is whether there is a need for women on an SF A-team. One possible answer to this could be an old SF experimentation, called the Special Action Force (SAF).

The SAF[65] was a company of mixed specialists not found on an A-Team. Configurations of this company included detachments like PSYOP Teams, Veterinary teams, Military Police, Preventive Medicine, and Communication specialists for fixed installations. This company was regionally aligned and language-qualified. The 8th Special Forces Group was home to the SAF organization. The Group's mission was counterinsurgency in Latin America. The deploying SF team could add –bolt-ons" from that company much like the OSS concept. In essence, this was like a company team, purposely built for the mission. This would be a way of approaching the issue of women on the detachment.

Would a revisiting of the OSS structures be useful for the CIA and SOF for 21st century operations?

The short answer for the SOF community is yes. The OSS again was —prpose-built," flexible in design, and more autonomous than today. Part of this was due to the nature of the conflict and part was due to the technology of the times. Donovan's selection process

---

[63] From an interview with Billy Waugh in Las Vegas, 2004 printed in *The Interview*, December 2005. Master Sergeant (ret) Waugh is a veteran of both US Army Special Forces and the CIA.

[64] Troy, *The Office of Strategic Services: America's First Intelligence Agency.*

[65] The 8th Special Forces Group, D Company, from 1963 to1972 contained a Special Action Force (SAF), Military Police (MP), Military Intelligence (MI), Medical, Engineers, PSYOP and Security Agency detachments. Its primary mission was counterinsurgency in Latin America. SAF was also defined in Army Field Manual 31-21, –Special Action Force (SAF)," February 1969. —The SAF is a specially trained, area oriented, partially language-qualified, ready force, available to the commander of a unified command for the support of cold, limited, and general war operations. SAF organizations may vary in size and capabilities according to theater requirements."

stressed the idea that the field personnel were expected to make decisions or actions without lots of guidance as long as it advanced the End State of winning the war.

The accountability of funding had limited visibility and oversight. This is enjoyed by the CIA more so than USSOCOM. The resourcing and authorities reports address this in more detail. The bottom line is there is a need for more flexibility in the resourcing authorities.

As discussed earlier, aviation is an area that should be explored with the new SOF Aviation Command. How much UAV and other air assets can the SF Groups count on to be at least placed under their tactical control (TACON)?

Integration of SOF organization in support of specific missions should be re-examined. To be sure there is a long history of Command and Control configurations (Combined Joint Special Operations Task Force, Joint Special Operations Task Force, Joint Psychological Operations Task Force, and Special Operations Command and Control Element, as examples). One idea developed as part of the investigation of SOF integration into the Future Force dealt with Special Operations Command and Control Element (SOCCE). The idea[66] was to establish a cadre of SF Officers and NCOs in regionally focused, rapidly deployable teams (SOCCE) from LNO duty with conventional Units of Action (UA), today called Brigade Combat Teams (BCTs). These teams would be made up of SF soldiers who have returned from an overseas deployment waiting schooling (Staff College) or a new assignment. They would be controlled by USASOC to manage them.

Another intriguing idea relates to the OSS economic war. This was an attack or at least leveraging of networks to influence outcomes. Clearly, we have some efforts along this same line, for example, ―following the money‖[67] as a key component of threat financial analysis. However, this has been a reactive approach to a specific problem. The OSS started from a system approach: how does it work, and can it be influenced for a specific outcome? This approach is more indirect as opposed to direct action on a specific source of funding (drug lords) or source of revenue (drug supplies).

Currently, our use of money as bullets has not been effective in the current fight. Title 22 funding has been more about spending than producing a desired or effective result. This lack of effectiveness is a symptom of poor integrated planning between the

---

[66] JSOU Senior Fellow comments from personal experience as USAJFKSWCS liaison to the U.S. Army's Unit of Action (UA) Battle Lab from 2003 to 2005.

[67] Wesley J.L. Andersen, *Disrupting Threat Finances*, JSOU Report 08-3 (Hurlburt Field, FL: JSOU Press, April 2008).

host nation and supporting countries. The lack of understanding of the Internal Defense and Development (IDAD)[68] model is one reason for this lack of coordination. Insurgent warfare is about legitimacy or governance. This means more focus on indirect action and less on direct action. The U.S. Air Force recently circulated a draft of IDAD, which once was a major part of SF education. This suggests that a review of operational needs should be linked to curriculum review to determine if SOF education needs an update.

Does either the CIA or SOF need new authorities to bring experts (regional, cultural, linguistic) into the service for short periods of time at a senior grade to support missions?

The OSS had many advantages that are not present today. The pool of candidates available to them was large. A national draft for the military was underway and continued throughout the war. The national will was focused on the outcome of the war, and the country was totally committed and engaged. The OSS looked good as a patriotic means to support the war effort for those who either had been educated overseas, or traveled extensively abroad and had linguistic skills that went beyond the high school and college levels of language training. This meant that much of the initial crop of OSS members were from well-to-do families. As the war went on, first generation Americans were recruited to further capitalize on their culture, language and regional knowledge. More importantly, was their willingness to think beyond the same target audience as the conventional military. They looked to people older than 39 and were gender-blind. This allowed them a resource pool that was broader than the military needed. They sought experienced and knowledgeable personnel rather than just physically fit personnel.

The Research and Analysis Branch was filled with many of the best minds in the country coming from academia, business and industry. Donovan believed that OSS volunteers needed to come to the fight ready, not prepared to be trained to fight. The R&A experts brought with them knowledge and networks from their civilian work ready to fight. This afforded the operators in the field insights that they would have had to learn on their own (reach back). The OSS was about influence and leveraging networks, which came from the highest levels of the society. The R&A team had both influence from their

---

[68] Joint Publication JP-3-24, "Counter Insurgency Operations," October 2009. Internal Defense and Development (IDAD) is defined as follows: "The full range of measures taken by a nation to promote its growth and to protect itself from subversion, lawlessness, and insurgency. It focuses on building viable institutions (political, economic, social, and military) that respond to the needs of society, also called IDAD." Also see Joint Publication JP 3-22, "Foreign Internal Defense," July 2010. It contains a chart depicting IDAD Strategy, page IV-5, figure IV-2.

former jobs and networks that were developed over a longer life than the 18-year-old draftee.

The wartime legislation and demand for skill supported Donovan's needs. The general assumption of authority and absence of oversight allowed for less scrutiny in some areas. The initial phase of working out of the White House and using the President's funds kept the bureaucrats at bay. By the same token, it created enemies in areas that needed or would need support to achieve the OSS goals.

Current Organization

USASOC/JFKSWCS does not have all the advantages of the OSS. It does have some, and the current levels of authority seem sufficient to meet the current needs. The Authorities Report will explore this in more detail. However, it is clear there are some disadvantages.

The MAVNI recruitment program was created after 9/11 to address a critical need for people knowledgeable in certain languages. The program is healthcare-focused (doctors and nurses), but USSOCOM has some 92 personnel in the command that are a product of this program. The primary shortcoming is obtaining security clearances on a timely basis. USSOCOM needs these people in sensitive areas, and the delay in obtaining their required clearance has reduced the effectiveness of the program. The delays are caused by the lack of proper vetting from the country of origin.

What USSOCOM needs is something like the Lodge Act of 1950 (1950-1959), to be able to recruit persons that meet our needs for cultural awareness, advanced language proficiency, and political and geographic knowledge of key regions. There appears to be a need that goes beyond ―gray beard" contractors and a cultural need for uniformed personnel. ―Took a lot of time to distinguish between training and education in preparing SOF. — Afghan veteran"[69]

As suggested within this section, there may be other authorities to permit NCOs to fly (UAV or aircraft), add additional manpower (cyber warriors) and structure (SAF) that will require examination. The resourcing and authority section will touch on some of these points.

Are there new authorities required to achieve your recommendations?

_____

[69] JSOU Report, *OSS Report, Irregular Warfare and the OSS Model*, 2-4 Nov 2009, ISBN 1-93374-45-8 (Hurlburt Field, FL: JSOU Press, 2010).

See above and sections on resourcing and authorities for more information.

Will there be new levels of resourcing required (not numbers of dollars rather a description of resources-education, enablers, equipment…)?

This answer, of course, will depend on what is changed. For example, if a SAF unit is created for forward deployed SF Battalions, it will have an impact on the TO&E of the SF organization, on facilities, education/training and other expenditures.

Cyber Warfare positions would require more specialized equipment, increased training and a probably more computer and other electronics savvy SF type soldiers.

Economic Warfare would require course development to produce more experienced and highly educated economists or finance persons. The duty position probably would be at Group or Theater Special Operations Command (TSOC) level to be the most effective—regional impact, not local level.

Recommendations:

O-1: Review OSS MO with the current MISO and CA structures to determine ways to increase team integration from the planning to execution and synchronization with SF units on a regional orientation.

O-2: Consider on-the-job training approach to increase CA skills for selected areas (sewage treatment plant operations) similar to the concept employed by SF medics.

O-3: Review the OSS employment of women in operations to the current gender restrictions on all SOF organizations to determine if any modifications are required.

O-4: Conduct a review of a SF concept of SAF (bolt-ons) structure to enhance the forward-deployed SF battalions in order to increase capabilities and unit cohesion in regional operations.

O-5: Review IATF plans to determine other ways to leverage economic tools (follow the money) in the current fight against terrorism by considering how the OSS employed their economic warfare organizations.

O-6: Conduct curriculum review of SOF education to determine relevance to the Core Activities and current operations.

O-7: Examine existing programs with OSS practices to bring native speakers into the program with the need for security clearances in order to employ their skills more quickly into the fight.

Resourcing

This section summarizes research and findings on the OSS approach toward allocating resources and the current approach employed by U.S. Special Forces and the CIA. It will offer some recommendations for application as it relates to the future of U.S. Special Operations Forces. Judgments expressed are drawn from reading OSS-related literature, discussions with military officers, civilian leaders, and a historian at the CIA. A set of Study Questions were developed to guide and trigger discussion intended to yield concrete recommendations.

Before addressing the study questions directly, it is useful to review some observations with regard to the OSS approach to allocating resources based on input from Mr. Rob Townley,[70] an OSS historian and ―The War Report of the OSS" by Peter Karlow.[71]

The OSS‗s Special Funds branch was responsible for financing the secret activities of OSS through ―unvouchered funds." Such funds were necessary to the maintenance of cover, whether of a corporation, a training installation, a recruiting office, or an agent or group of agents in enemy or enemy-occupied territory. The use of unvouchered funds supported the most secret operations in which OSS engaged, and the Special Funds branch spent a great deal of time acquiring stockpiles of foreign currency for use in those operations. Unvouchered funds are moneys made available to the President by Congress to support activities of a confidential nature, are exempt from the provisions of public law regulating the outlay of government funds, and not comprehensively audited.[72]

When the Coordinator of Information was established under the direction of Major General Donavan, its original unvouchered funds were allotted from the President's Emergency Fund in September 1941, the first allocation being $100,000. After the creation of OSS in June 1942, an additional appropriation of $3,000,000 was granted for the fiscal year (1942-1943). A second allotment in the amount of approximately $10,000,000 was further supplied for the same period. In the spring of 1943 the OSS was ultimately able to go before Congress and obtain directly its own appropriation for the fiscal year 1943-1944. This appropriation was granted in the amount of $21,000,000, of

---

[70] Rob Townley, December 2010.

[71] Peter Karlow, *The Overseas Targets: War Report of the OSS (Office of Strategic Services) Volume II* (Washington, D.C.: the Walker Publishing Company, 1976).

[72] Michael Warner, ―COI Came First" *The Office of Strategic Services: America's First Intelligence Agency* (e-book). Center for the Study of Intelligence, Central Intelligence Agency, 15 March 2007; available at https://www.cia.gov/library/center-for-the-study-of-intelligence/csi-publications/books-and-monographs/oss/art02.htm; accessed December 2011.

which approximately $15,000,000 was classified as unvouchered funds. In fiscal year 1944-1945, Congress appropriated $57,000,000[73] ($57 million in 1945 dollars is roughly equivalent to $691 million in today's dollars).

According to the National War Agencies Appropriation Bill of 1945[74], expenditures had only to be endorsed by Donovan and submitted to the Treasury Department to secure reimbursement for amounts disbursed from Special Funds. This departure from the normal Congressional requirement of detailed accounting for government expenditures was necessary for OSS security. Later the process included routing through the Joint Staff, but only as a courtesy.[75]

There were a few driving forces behind the way the OSS resourced its operations. Resources were dedicated to an activity based largely on its return on investment ratio— the activities with the most disproportionate effect in comparison to the amount of funds expended on the activity won out, hands down, nearly every time. The J8 equivalents of the WWII era did not judge the merit of a sustained operation based on its parts and objective, rather operations were judged based on what they delivered. Just because something is inexpensive does not mean it is ineffective. Work backward from effect in the analysis of resource allocation, and you have a far better means of judging what to keep and what to toss.

The entire operating mantra of the OSS was different than ours is today, and it shows through in the amount of resources we dedicate to certain things without thinking about our actions in the aggregate and how inane they can be sometimes. It can be boiled down to the supposition that the OSS, as a culture, knew how to _manage' the chessboard upon which it operated rather than chasing its adversaries this way and that as we are prone to do today. The ability to manage the operational environment, rather than just existing as a player within it, allows for far more efficient options to expend resources than does the latter option.

The OSS expended its resources with great care that they be spent on leveraging other existing networks or resource pools. The OSS never operated in a vacuum because it did not have the budget. Whereas, currently, we spend most of our time acting like we're alone with an opponent in a boxing ring, generating whatever punching power we

---

[73] David H. Berger, "The Use of Covert Paramilitary Activity as a Policy Tool: An Analysis of Operations Conducted by the United States Central Intelligence Agency, 1949-1951," (May 1995, Quantico VA) available at http://www fas.org/irp/eprint/berger.htm, accessed December 2010.
[74] Federal Records of World War II, Volume II, Military Records, Part One, Interallied and Interservice Military Agencies, section on The Office of Strategic Services.
[75] David H. Berger, 1995.

can just from our shoulder, what the OSS did took advantage of all other sources of force or momentum available inside that ring or out. Even if it meant paying the brute in the audience $20 to step in the ring and knock an opponent senseless, they would do it.

The OSS was created as a response to a national or even a global threat. Its creation was akin to someone _breaking the emergency glass' that you only do as a last resort, so as a service the OSS had a lot of ground to cover and little time to cover it. Thankfully, General Donovan had done much of the necessary work in the late 1930s to take some of the pressure off. Had this not been done, the resources that the OSS expended would not have been anywhere near as effective. So you have to view the lifespan of OSS as part of a continuum. This circumstance supports the position that it is more cost effective to maintain a low level presence in many areas of the world in order to help manage conflict rather than having to react to it. The activities that happened before the OSS was created are good examples of how this philosophy is effective and saves money.

Summary of Group Study:

1. What are critical resourcing issues for CIA and SOF today (manpower, education, training, equipment)?

The critical resourcing issues will revolve around overcoming parochial inter-service/interagency rivalries, not doctrine, organization, training, materiel, leadership and education, personnel, and facilities (DOTMLPF) or appropriation funding. USSOCOM was neither intended, nor funded, to function independently and was designed to rely on service support. It is the statutory responsibility of the services to provide department-common capabilities to SOF. Currently, Major Force Program 11 (MFP-11) resources are intended to fund SOF-peculiar requirements. Obtaining broad agreement and support on SOF-peculiar and service-common is often a challenge. Tackling drastic USSOCOM reorganization that potentially requires additional inter-service/interagency support, funding, and authorities will be monumental when leveraging status quo is already difficult.

Manpower is a problem because there is not enough SOF to go around. The biggest problem in manpower is non-SOF enabler support. SOF goes through significant efforts to recruit and train the best SOF operators but fills non-SOF-billets generally with what the services provide (with exception for some specific units that do selection support MOSs). SOF is not able to select the right enabler and support personnel, but these positions are critical to SOF success.

As we attempt to grow SOF to meet demand, there is a danger of diluting the force with —acceptable" operators to meet the numbers demand instead of the —best" operators we need to accomplish strategically important missions. We need to break the service norms of a —career path" to provide our senior operators experiences needed to further develop SOF. Currently, we need to follow service-acceptable career paths to ensure advancement. These career paths do not equate to the desired SOF experience.

In education, language training needs to be more developed so it is enduring throughout a SOF operator's career and follows him wherever he goes. Some forces have very effective initial language training, but sustainment and improvement away from tactical units is difficult. SOF operators should have language training requirements to meet even when they leave a tactical unit to maintain or improve their proficiency because it is too late to do when they return to a tactical unit.

The disconnect between the TSOC that commands and controls SOF and the components that provide the trained and equipped SOF is the biggest issue in resourcing equipment. Since the components are not in the fight, they are naturally behind when it comes to developing the next equipment capability. There needs to be a tighter, more agile loop from identifying a requirement forward and resourcing a solution for the force. The constant challenge is keeping pace with technology while preserving MFP-11 buying power.

How was the OSS resourced as a percent of war budget? What problems did they face in resourcing during the war?

The OSS was a very small percent of the war budget. It is difficult to aggregate, but as noted earlier, for fiscal year 1944-1945, $57 million was appropriated by Congress for the OSS while in 1944, the U.S. defense budget topped out at $85 billion.

Overall, the OSS was well resourced during the war. There was some fraud, waste and abuse. It is almost unavoidable that the more flexibility and speed an organization has to use funds the more chance there is for abuse. The OSS was far to one end of this scale where they had maximum speed and flexibility with funds, but they were at high risk for waste.

If the CIA and SOF were reorganized, what types of resourcing issues would be envisioned?

This is a complex question and would involve a study by itself. It is not an organization issue as much as a utilization/employment issue. SOF is a strategic asset and should be used accordingly. The SOF focus should be on the *prevent and deter* phases of conflict, not getting bogged down in the current fight. The challenge is defining success to the policy makers. Essentially, success of SOF would mean not having to escalate to the use of kinetic force. In other words, if —nothing happens" in the region in which we are employed we are a success. It is difficult to convince the policy makers to spend money for —nothing." Regardless, our current employment in Afghanistan is not optimized. We are not getting the return on investment that we could if we were utilized properly.

A significant resourcing issue would be the difference between USSOCOM funding and service funding. USSOCOM could do reorganization that required USSOCOM funds only, but would have to get support from the services to make changes that required any service funds or resources. If the changes required more or different personnel, then it would be critical to ensure the changes are feasible for the services to support.

The current force provider/force employer model should be studied to consider alternatives. There are certain SOF units that operate on a different model where the same headquarters is responsible for garrison command and control (C2) and training but also commands and controls the force in combat. This model provides much greater agility in resourcing combat needs with units or equipment, but also makes the combat headquarters consider the long-term health of the force when making requests. The current system where the TSOC employs SOF and the component provides them was not developed for today's environment of continuous combat. SOF should consider other models to see if there are more efficient methods, but a change to this system would have significant resourcing impacts, and a full study of the DOTMLPF impacts would need to be considered.

USSOCOM has little to no relief from Department of Defense-imposed statutes, regulations, and oversight that limit its agility. The regulatory requirements drive USSOCOM to invest in large bureaucratic —Service-like" organizational structures with all the associated inefficiencies, particularly in the execution of the Title X roles and responsibilities. Statutes, policies, and regulations, which if removed, would allow greater efficiencies.

If either CIA or SOF obtained new authorities for bringing experts (regional, cultural, linguistic) into the service for short periods of time at a senior grade to support missions, what resources would be required?

Special authorities from the Department of Defense (DOD) may be required to hire an assortment of experts for short periods of time, with the flexibility to let them go without incurring a career or long-term employee status (similar to contractors, but with rank and authority to represent USSOCOM).

The OSS had to hire experts because they did not have time to develop their own expertise in many cases. Similarly, USSOCOM will face challenges that it could address quicker by hiring some experts either until USSOCOM can develop its own experts (which would involve education) for enduring issues or until the expert is no longer required for specific topics. This practice should not be overused to prevent causing the same level of mistrust that existed between the OSS ground operatives and the largely civilian-oriented headquarters back in the U.S. Additionally, any experts hired should be used only in their field of expertise and not used for leadership positions.

Special allowances would have to be made to match or compensate said personnel for the loss in terms of personal remuneration they may endure by signing on with the service (salary matching, compensation schemes, etc.). Real talent is not cheap.

Issues of association, such experts may lose legitimacy in their respective professional communities if it is publicly known that they are taking on a position with the government. There may need to be a mechanism in place to engage such talent in an indirect fashion (CIA already does this).

An alternative to bringing experts into the service would be to capitalize on our organic SOF operators by sending them to advanced regional, cultural, and linguistic schools. We need to invest in talent management and develop a human capital plan. We must source our ―Lawrence of Arabia‖ strategy, not outsource it. It is more efficient and arguably more effective to provide SOF operators with advanced education and return them to the force instead of hiring non-military personnel for potential tactical employment with regional impact.

Are there new authorities required to achieve your recommendations?
Maybe, but most of the necessary changes are not in authorities, they are in procedure. Legislative armed services committees would be required to write such procedural changes into law at some point, but they may not need to initially to get things started.

If new authorities are required, a more detailed analysis would need to be done to determine what advantage bringing a person on to active service has over contracting them or employing them as a government civilian. The discriminators are likely to be speed of hiring and the ability to hire someone into a senior position/rank.

Will there be new levels of resourcing required (not numbers of dollars rather a description of resources-education, enablers, equipment…)?
No, additional resources should not be required except perhaps in the requirement for non-organic General Purpose Forces enablers, but they should be a service bill. There will need to be reallocation of resources within the existing budget, not new levels. USSOCOM's budget is more than adequate to accomplish the mission. There is a great deal of redundancy to be found within the current structure that could be turned into operational or training capacity necessary to bring on new talent. The new talent would be brought into the service for the expertise they already possess; therefore, they should require only some basic military training like those individuals brought into the OSS.

We need less Congressional oversight and more flexibility with existing resources. We need a ―cash-like" account that can be used for operations and maintenance (O&M), procurement, or research, development, test and evaluation (RDT&E) to resource in support of the fight, similar to a combat mission needs statement (CMNS) pot of money for the USSOCOM Commander to use in a rapid fashion. Right now, we have the purple (MFP-11) pot, but it is not considered rapidly available funds; it is normal program objective memorandum process funds.

Recommendations:

R1. Concentrate resources on persistent engagement activities in order to ―manage" the global environment.

R2. Enable SOF to operate with colorless (e.g., DERF) funding to reduce overhead and increase USSOCOM‗s ability to meet urgent needs similar to OSS‗s unvouchered funds.

R3. Tailor DOD oversight; manage as a Special Activity with ―Special Funds" vice a service-like entity by reducing numbers of reviews, reports, and decision layers.

R4. Create a human capital plan (talent management plan) to develop the regional, cultural, and linguistic expertise of our organic SOF operators and enablers.

R5. Transition SOF acquisitions to become service-common programs to reduce overall equipping, training, and support costs.

Authorities

This section summarizes research and findings on the OSS authorities and their approach to resource authorities and allocation. It will highlight the current authorities granted to SOF, the CIA, and their authorities, which are also many times tied to resourcing. The summary will offer some recommendations for application as it relates to the future of U.S. Special Operations Forces. Judgments expressed are drawn from reading OSS-related literature, discussions with military officers and civilian leaders from the office of the DASD/SO/CT, USASOC and OSS historians, and former officers at the CIA. A set of study questions were developed to guide and trigger discussion intended to yield concrete recommendations.

─A good idea without funding is a hallucination." -Anonymous Staff Officer

What is legal authority, and why is it important? Funding and resourcing are tied to legal authority. According to the Judge Advocate General's Operational Law Handbook, the expenditure of appropriated funds is governed by the established rule that ─the expenditure of public funds is proper only when authorized by Congress, not that proper funds may be expended unless prohibited by Congress." Congress defines legal authorities via several means to include: U.S. Code Title 10, U.S. Code Title 22, DOD Authorizations Acts, and DOD appropriations. Federal agencies also provide guidance through regulations and Comptroller General Decision.[76]

Without a clear legal authority, one must be prepared to articulate a rationale for an expenditure which is ─necessary and incident" to an existing authority. Executing appropriated funds without proper legal authority can lead to what is known as a Purpose violation. Failure to correct a purpose violation obligation (of funds) can lead to a violation of the amount which will in turn cause an Anti-Deficiency Act Violation. In addition to all this legal jargon, more legal jargon translated below explains that Congress imposes fiscal controls through three basic mechanisms, (each implemented by one or more statutes):

- Proper Purpose. Expenditures must be authorized by law for the intended purpose.
- Time Limits. Appropriations have a life span, and must be used during their period of availability.

---

[76] Definition of Legal Authority, posted by USSOCOM Special Operations Financial Management SOFM-M policy, and derived from Chapter 16 of the Judge Advocate General's Legal Center and School, Operational Law Handbook, (2010, MacDill Air Force base, FL).

• Obligations must be within the amounts authorized by Congress.[77]

Without delving deeper into law, it is clear to see how today's SOF operator must also be well versed in what is and is not authorized. USSOCOM has a —one-stop shopping" portal for its staff to research authorities and what type of funding is required for tasks. In that portal there is an —authorities matrix" containing detailed information on more than 40 authorities that relate to Special Forces Activities, training, contingency operations, and humanitarian operations. A few examples of the authorities listed are Section 1206/1207/1208 Authorities, Combating Terrorism Fellowship Program, and Contingency Construction Authority.[78] A vast difference from what the OSS was saddled with during WWII. For example, the Operational Groups Field Manual, a 31-page manual used by the OSS references JCS Directive 155/11/D for its authority to —execute independent operations against enemy targets."[79] The JCS directive that delineated the functions and authorities of the OSS was a document of only six pages.[80]

What are the authorities for the establishment of the CIA and Special Operations Forces today? How do they link to each other? Are the authorities sufficient to achieve their mutual tasks?

Bottom line: Overarching authorities come from civilian and political leadership—primarily the Executive Branch and more importantly Congress, since it controls the purse strings. Authorities can be granted and expanded OR retracted and taken away altogether by statutes, regulations, policies, and executive orders.

President Harry Truman, by executive order deactivated the OSS in 1945 and split its activities up between the Department of State and Department of War. The 1947 National Securities Act created a new clandestine agency to replace the OSS: the CIA.[81] By contrast, due to perceived military parochialism, Congress forced the Department of Defense into action with the 1986 Cohen-Nunn Amendment to the Goldwater-Nichols

---

[77] USSOCOM Special Operations Financial Management SOFM-M policy, and derived from Chapter 16 of the Judge Advocate General's Legal Center and School, Operational Law Handbook, (2010, MacDill Air Force Base, FL).

[78] —New Matrix Puts Funding Authorities at Your Finger Tips," policy article from the USSOCOM Spear Policy Newsletter, November 2010, (2010, MacDill Air Force Base, FL), p. 3.

[79] Office of Strategic Services Field Manual No. 6, —Operational Group Field Manual - Strategic Services (Provisional)," 25 April 1944, declassified on March 12, 2009, National Archives Record Service (NARS).

[80] Joint Chiefs of Staff (JCS) Directive 155/11/D, —Functions of the Office of Strategic Services," 27 October 1943, declassified on September 20, 1995, National Archives Record Service (NARS).

[81] Michael Warner, —An End and a Beginning." *The Office of Strategic Services: America's First Intelligence Agency* (e-book), 2007.

Act. President Reagan signed it into law in 1987 to establish USSOCOM. USSOCOM acts as a unified combatant command with service-like authorities with MFP-11 funding authority. Since 9/11 it has also evolved into the lead command in synchronizing plans for global operations against terrorist networks.[82] One critical shortfall is that USSOCOM was not originally intended, nor funded to function independently, and was designed to rely on other military services support. MFP-11 funds are intended to fund SOF-peculiar requirements. Obtaining broad agreement and support on SOF-peculiar and service-common requirements is often a challenge.

USSOCOM, in contrast to the OSS and the CIA, was not envisioned to conduct clandestine, strategic, or operational intelligence operations. USSOCOM missions referred to as —SOFCore Activities"[83] include direct action (DA), special reconnaissance, UW, FID, CA, counterterrorism (CT), MISO, information operation (IO), counterproliferation of weapons of mass destruction (WMD), security force assistance (SFA), counterinsurgency operations (COIN), and any activities specified by the President or Secretary of Defense. Note that special reconnaissance is not considered intelligence collection. Most SOF units have a competence and charter to carry out several to all of the core SOF activities while some specialize.

The _National Commission on Terrorist Attacks Upon the United States‘ also known as the 9/11 Commission report recommended expanding the role of USSOCOM. Recommendation 31 stated that —theCIA should retain responsibility and execution of clandestine and covert operations..." That recommendation led into the next with —however, that one important area of responsibility should change...[recommendation 32] The lead responsibility for directing and executing paramilitary operations, whether clandestine or covert, should shift to the Defense Department. There it should be consolidated with the capabilities for training, direction, and execution of such operations already being developed in the Special Operations Command."[84] Currently there is no SOF Doctrine[85] to address these specific concerns, and Recommendation 32 has not been

---

[82] U.S Special Operations Hand Book (2011), produced by USSOCOM Public Affairs, Mac Dill Air Force Base, FL: pg. 7-9.

[83] The 11 SOF core activities (—ay activities specified by the President and SECDEF is not counted") were accepted nomenclature until August 2011 when they were changed to Core Missions and Activities.

[84] Wording of Recommendation 32 from the report, available at http://9-11commission.gov/.

[85] In joint doctrine, Joint Publication 3-05 for Special Operations (April 2011) does not address it directly but states that the Department of Defense may be placed in a —supporting role to inter-organizational partners." USSOCOM SOF Publication 1, —SOF Dctrine" (August 2011) also does not directly address this issue. Both documents were in draft form during the study.

approved despite a presidential directed review of policy.[86] Expanding USSOCOM role in covert or clandestine mission areas will also raise additional legal concerns beyond the scope of this study.

Today, USSOCOM, as a service-like command, is authorized its own major force program (MFP-11), with all of the oversight any service budget would receive from Congress. In reference whether authorities are sufficient for either the CIA or SOF in comparison to the OSS, Lieutenant Colonel Steve Gregg in his research placed this into context:

> Since the disestablishment of the OSS, America's social and political environment changed in ways that leaders of the OSS would probably find both counterproductive and ironically appealing. Some of the most significant changes [reference to oversight of CIA clandestine and covert operations] were the findings of the 1976 Church Committee regarding paramilitary operations. These findings resulted in increased oversight of covert operations by Congress and more scrutiny over funds for clandestine organizations. In contrast, the leaders of the OSS might find the 1987 Nunn-Cohen Amendment to the Goldwater-Nichols Act a realization of their goals of a separate, national-level special operations capability. However, they would probably find the subordination of control and employment of special operations to geographical commanders troublesome at best.[87]

What were the authorities for the OSS and were they sufficient for their tasks? How did they support the military and other security organizations during the war?
Current laws and statutes regarding authorities, funding, and oversight of special operations, covert operations, and clandestine intelligence operations, are vastly different and more restrictive than the funding of the OSS. Congress exercised little or no oversight in the use of unvouchered funds, and Donovan personally had ―unprecedented access" to and support from the President."[88]

The OSS operated under broad and powerful authorities to ―collect and analyze strategic information" and to ―pla and operate…special services." The OSS also had

---

[86] ―Special Operations Forces (SOF) and CIA Paramilitary Operations issues for Congress," Congressional Research Service (CRS) Report for Congress, Order Code RS22017, Library of Congress, January 2005, updated December 2006, available at http://www.fas.org/sgp/crs/intel/RS22017.pdf.
[87] Steven C. Gregg, Major, USAF, ―Lessons of the OSS: Warnings and Guideposts for Modern SOF." (Air University, 2007), p. 15.
[88] Ibid, p. 2.

authorized responsibility for being in charge of resistance.[89] With such a broad mandate, the OSS was mostly free to operate as it saw fit to accomplish its mission.

Many of the OSS's greatest successes were in how it supported the military during the war. The OSS provided intelligence and assisted conventional forces by conducting sabotage to degrade and disrupt enemy units' morale and will to fight prior to engaging allied military units or during their efforts to withdraw. Intelligence included providing enemy order of battle information, such as the case where the OSS provided the location of the German 7th Corps Headquarters so it could be strafed.[90] The OSS also employed the resistance to attack a Panzer Division en-route to Normandy so it arrived with only 3,500 of 10,000 men and all on foot with no tanks or artillery because of attacks from guerrillas.[91] General Eisenhower said ―I consider that the disruption of enemy rail communication, the harassing of German road moves, and the continual and increasing strain placed on the German war economy and internal services throughout occupied Europe by the organized forces of the resistance played a very considerable part in our victory."[92] Lieutenant General A.M. Patch said, ―During the planning phase for our landing in southern France we were constantly kept informed of the enemy's strength and activities by American agents behind the lines."[93]

What is the process to make changes in the structure today for USSOCOM and CIA?

To make a change at USSOCOM or down to the division level, a request has to be submitted to the Special Operations Command Requirements Evaluation Board (SOCREB) for Deputy Combatant Commander approval. Three documents are included in the package: a doctrine, organizational, training, materiel, leadership and education, personnel, facilities change recommendation, a capability decision memorandum signed by the director or deputy director supporting the change, and a SOCREB briefing. To make a change to an organization below division level the same packet must be submitted to the SOCREB but then must also go through the applicable service organizational change process.

---

[89] Stewart Alsop and Thomas Braden, *Sub Rosa: The OSS and American Espionage* (New York: Reynal & Hitchcock, 1946), p. 13.

[90] Ibid., p. 5.

[91] Ibid., p. 4.

[92] Ibid., p. 5.

[93] Ibid., p. 5.

Structural changes will require Congressional approval or oversight. For example the Post 9/11, Intelligence Reform and Terrorism Prevention Act (IRTPA) - Public Law 108-458 delineates that procedures for operational coordination between DOD and CIA at minimum will provide: "methods of communication" between the SECDEF and Director, CIA; and when "conducting separate missions in the same geographic area, a mutual agreement on the tactical and strategic objectives for the region and a clear delineation of operational responsibilities."[94]

Are there existing authorities to bring line officers (not medical or legal) directly into the services at the rank of LTC or above? How was this done by the OSS? Is it a tool that would be useful to USSOCOM?

Many in USSOCOM agree that it can become a more agile force if it could bring experts into service to address specific problem sets. It takes time to grow experts, and if it is a discrete problem that does not require an enduring capability, then creating USSOCOM-internal experts is not efficient. The OSS had the ability to "hire" experts, the Group of 300, for example, because they did not have time to develop their own expertise in many cases. The OSS also operated during the "draft era" and the whole nation was mobilized and motivated to support the war effort. Direct commissions given in the OSS were a point of contention with many career military officers in and outside the OSS.

USSOCOM will face challenges that it could address quickly by hiring experts either until USSOCOM can develop its own experts for enduring issues or until those experts are no longer required for specific topics. The majority of officers contributing to this study warned that this practice should not be overused to prevent causing the same level of mistrust that existed between the OSS ground operatives and the largely civilian-oriented headquarters back in the U.S. Additionally, any experts hired should be used only in their field of expertise and not used for leadership positions. The MAVNI pilot program that permits non-citizens legally residing in the U.S. to join the military and quickly obtain citizenship has met with mixed reviews primarily due to the applicants not being able to pass the required security background checks.[95]

Some study participants questioned outright the validity of bringing outside experts and "putting rank on them." One recommendation is to in-source vice out-source our

---

[94] Delineated in Section 1013 "Joint Procedures for Operational Coordination between Department of Defense and Central Intelligence Agency," available at www.nctc.gov/docs/pl108_458.pdf , accessed December 2010.
[95] According to input from the USSOCOM J1 OSS study participants.

―Lawrence of Arabia strategy" by sending some of our SOF operators out to develop and hone required cultural and language skill sets. Also, in this day and age of heightened transparency it may be wiser to bring renowned experts discretely into the fold without enlisting them or providing direct commissions into uniformed service. The commissioned expert may lose legitimacy in his/her respective professional communities if it is made known publicly that they are now in uniform. The CIA uses this discrete and indirect method of hiring experts. One modern day example where the U.S. Army brought in experts without extending field grade rank is in the area of human terrain mapping. One assumption for direct commissioning at any level of rank would be that the new authority would have to be faster and easier to accomplish than contracting or hiring civil service civilians, or the authority would not be worthwhile. Regardless, the discriminator may likely be speed of hiring a subject matter expert due to a crisis or pressing issue, for which a line commission may be inappropriate. Study group members indicated that the authority for bringing someone onto active service via direct commission as field grade or above officers does not exist other than in the medical and legal career fields.

During WWII, the OSS commissioned personnel from early 1942 to 1945, and commissions were implied to be for the duration of the war and not to last more than 6 months following its conclusion. The JCS also gave the OSS the authority to commission without any basic training. However, even with a global war and more than 12 million serving in uniform, direct commissioning of civilians was a rare exception. The majority of those commissioned entered the Army Specialist Corps, and not the Regular Army. The other source was from commissioning enlisted to officer. The OSS was given an officer allotment from each of the military services. If requested the OSS could direct commission against these quotas as per Army Regulation 605-10, 10 December 1941. OSS commissions also did not count against TO&E stateside or in theater. [96]

The OSS used direct commissions primarily for three reasons. The first was to protect civilian personnel of draft age who were already with the COI or OSS from being drafted into the other services. The second was to allow enlisted soldiers to achieve parity with British counterparts in enemy occupied territory, since the British policy was to commission their enlisted in order to put the lower ranking U.S. personnel at higher risk. Lastly, OSS civilian subject matter experts (SMEs) who were later inserted behind enemy lines to deal with military occupation issues were commissioned through Military Government (today's Civil Affairs). One example of this was the Monument and Fine

---

[96] Troy Sacquety, discussion and email input from the USASOC Historian, January 2011.

Arts Commission whose task was to preserve European history and artifacts. U.S. citizens and later citizens of partner nations were commissioned, and the Commanding Officer in Theater had commissioning authority. Despite the expedient manner in which direct commissions were accomplished during the war, there were troublesome issues that developed since no long-term plan was developed by the OSS. Difficulties with promotions did arise due to the TO&E exceptions and recognition during separations were also upsetting to many OSS veterans.[97] According to the USASOC historian it is an unknown whether OSS personnel could have performed many of their duties out of uniform.

Other examples brought to the study group came from the Department of State (DOS) representative to the USSOCOM IATF. The DOS uses Title 5 authorities, and Personal Service Contracts (PSC) to bring SMEs and former DOS officials into the Foreign Service. Of interest is the PSC program where the individual SME is contracted directly by the DOS for up to 5 years to serve in overseas posts providing skills that may not exist there. The individual is treated similar to a Foreign Service Officer (FSO) and afforded all benefits except for participation in the Thrift Savings Plan. The Bureau for International Narcotics and Law Enforcement Affairs (INL) and embassy-based Narcotics Affairs Sections (NAS) have successfully used this program in employing former law enforcement and military (many are former SOF) experts to equip, train, and advise partner nations' law enforcement, paramilitary and military organizations engaged in counternarcotics activities. For USSOCOM the closest methods that can be used today are to hire civilians through contracting companies or by creating a civil service position. The DOS PSC concept removes the long and arduous process in hiring of civil service employees, and reduces the sometimes exorbitant costs that companies charge for an individual contractor's work. A more detailed analysis would need to be done to determine what benefit bringing a person into active duty service has over contracting them or employing them as a government civilian.

Are there new authorities required to achieve the recommendations?
Yes, but USSOCOM cannot do this right now on its own. Congressionally- and DoD-imposed statutes, regulations, and oversight mechanisms are not easily overturned, and many lawmakers would argue that they should not be. One commonly heard complaint of SOF operators at the tactical unit level starts with ―if we only had the authority to…" On

---

[97] Troy Sacquety, 2011.

the USSOCOM staff, "the angry Turks" (experienced SOF operators) have spearheaded other innovation groups and call for combining, streamlining, or doing away with oversight committees in order to become a more effective and efficient organization of SOF warriors. One suggestion from SF officers at Fort Bragg involved assigning more SOF operators to CIA where they would then be covered by less restrictive CIA authorities to carry out special operations and irregular activities. This blending of warrior capabilities under authorities more linked to the President of the United States would be reminiscent of the former OSS.

Will there be new levels of resourcing required (not numbers of dollars rather a description of resources-education, colors of money, equipment...)

If Recommendation 32 of the 9/11 Commission Report is to be enacted, new authorities and funding will have to be legislated. In reference to bringing in outside experts, the levels of resourcing should be fairly limited since they would be brought into service for expertise or a capability they already have, so they should need fairly little training other than some basic military training. There would be individual equipment requirements, but those are minimal in consideration of the amount of individual equipment already purchased annually. It would also require some type of training center to give the new people some minimal level of military training, much like doctors going through an Officer's Basic Course. There would have to be systems in place to incorporate them into the military personnel and health care systems. If the skill they were hired for required specific equipment that is not organic to SOF or the military already, then there would have to be funds to purchase the necessary equipment.

Recommendations to address authorities primarily rely on lobbying efforts to convince civilian leadership in OSD and Congress that USSOCOM is trustworthy enough to have less oversight. We should also be aware that the political will to make these changes must exist. Many could argue that in order to maintain American values, such as those that agree with the Church Committee findings, the "speed bumps" need to remain in place to prevent unauthorized military operations in variance of stated U.S. policy. Some of the recommendations for this group overlap with recommendations from the other study groups, primarily the Resourcing Group.

Recommendations

A1. Tailor DOD oversight; manage as a Special Activity with "Special Funds" vice a service-like entity by reducing numbers of reviews, reports, and decision layers.

A2. Develop Joint SOF Doctrine.

A3. Refocus and enhance 1206/1207/1208 Authorities. This will enable a more rapid ability to support partner nations.

A4. Enable SOF to operate with colorless funding (e.g. DERF) to reduce overhead and increase SOF's ability to meet urgent needs similar to the OSS unvouchered funds.

A5. Refine roles and responsibilities in synchronizing global operations.

A6. Increase authorities and roles in intelligence operations.

Annex A: Recommendations Chart

Recommendations made by each of the four (4) OSS Study Group reports (listed in each section) were discussed, debated, voted on, and synthesized at the January 2011 OSS Symposium where a final list was compiled. The explicit task presented by Admiral Olson was to document what could be accomplished within the Command (**internal actions**) and what recommendations required coordination or approval outside of USSOCOM (**external actions**). The chart below was developed to quickly depict those items and where the solutions lay (**internal, external, or both**). Several of these actions have occurred or are underway. This chart is an abstract of the final recommendations complied at the January 2011 symposium.

Recommendations	Internal Actions	External Actions
Selection		
Establish a selection process for non-operator (enablers) personnel.	**WHAT**: Critical to the support of SOF are those non-SOF assets that contribute to success (logistics, Admin), there is a need to identify and retain that group of personnel with in SOCOM. **HOW**: SOF leaders need to identify personnel that SOCOM should retain in the community.	**WHAT**: There is a need with in the personnel systems to enable SOCOM to identify and retain non-SOF personnel without causing harm to their careers if they stay too long in SOCOM. **HOW**: Provide the Services with a listing of critical non-SOF MOSs to determine a methodology how to share their services.
Target Recruitment efforts in ethnic neighborhoods and enclaves in the United States.	**WHAT**: SOCOM needs to anticipate future diversity needs from communities within the US as priority recruitment areas, as an example the 18L program. **HOW**: Identify those countries where SOCOM sees the greatest future needs for engagement; determine the language requirements and where they can be found in the U.S.	**WHAT**: DOD recruiting needs to review incentives for diversity groups to encourage their enlistment into SOF MOSs. There is a need to look more like the foreign nations that we operate in. **HOW:** Focus on incentives that appeal to people who are motivated to serve in areas where their language skills and cultural knowledge will benefit the nation
Build and maintain a SOF workforce that represents the rich diversity of the world	**WHAT:** In order to understand the complexity of the world, SOCOM needs a more diverse force that better appreciates the cultural environments it will operate in. Much like the OSS selecting 1st or 2nd	**WHAT:** DOD should continue to provide incentives for non-citizens and 1st or 2d generation to citizens to membership in the military and also in SOF

	generation citizen, SOCOM needs to embrace these groups. **HOW:** SOCOM identifies those areas in the world with a potential for crisis and identify those language and cultural skill necessary to engage in the solution.	organizations. **HOW:** Coordinate with SOCOM on the language and cultural skills required to support SOF needs for Persistent Engagement activities.
Introducing a new law similar to the Lodge (Bill) Act to encourage recent immigrants seeking U.S. citizenship through military service.	**WHAT:** SOCOM continues to support MAVNI Program as a short-term method of increasing diversity. There should also be an examination of how rapidly gain clearance for these individuals. **HOW:** Coordinate with the investigative services on ways to speed up the security clearance process.	**WHAT:** SOCOM, through DoD and SOLA, should suggest the enactment of a DREAM-like Act; it also suggests the need to enhance (funding) programs to have key personnel (18L/FAO) to study overseas to learn language and culture. **HOW:** Increase the resourcing to the existing program and expand the numbers of personnel selected for those programs. It may require a review of personnel promotion systems to prevent these specialists from being harmed for being in the program.
USSOCOM J-1 (Personnel) be granted authority to manage all personnel issues, including recruitment and selection for the entire force.	**WHAT:** SOCOM manage all SOCOM personnel activities (Service like responsibility); promotions, schooling, in order to retain personnel; protect them in the promotion system and identify personnel for schooling (JSOFSEA); investigate whether there is a need for a SOF Command & Staff Course like CGSC. **HOW:** Conduct a study how to best approach this issue and identify those areas that can quickly be implemented or reinforced (JSOFSEA) with a strategy of expanding gradually.	**WHAT:** DoD needs to formerly endorse the SOCOM personnel needs as different than the Services; JSOFSEA should be ratified by all the Services as the test case of this difference; support the investigation of post qualification education for SOF Warriors up to the 04/-5 level rather than meeting the requirements of the Services. **HOW:** Coordinate with SOCOM personnel and educators to determine what and how shifting of some Service responsibilities can be moved to SOCOM and present to the Service Chiefs.
Use a complete battery of psychological and aptitude assessments to	**WHAT:** The selection process has served the community well since the 1940's; however, warfare continues to change. The selection criteria should continue to be evaluated to ensure the process meets the	**WHAT:** Although, the SOF Service Components have some unique differences, there are some attributes that are common. SOF Components should seek

determine specific characteristics required for SOF.	SOF community's needs. **HOW**: Direct coordination between the SOF components to determine what needs to amended, added, or deleted to ensure the quality of SOF warriors remains high. (Some thought about adding a lie detector test.)	ways to synchronize the selection tests to determine what those characteristics are in order to have a clear picture of the SOF Warrior. **HOW:** Request Service assistance in the screening of SOF candidates by conducting the testing with SOF test standards.
Organization		
Conduct curriculum review of SOF education to determine relevance to the Core Activities and current operations.	**WHAT**: There is a need for a study of SOF Service Component Curriculum Review to determine if it is meeting the needs of the components and if there are common knowledge areas that can be standardized for all SOF Warriors (COIN is now a Core Activity again). **HOW:** Direct the SOF Service Components to Conduct a Curriculum Review, coordinate the results to identify areas that common.	
Consider On-the-job training approach to increase CA skills for selected areas (sewage treatment plant operations) similar to the concept employed by SF medics.	**WHAT**: The highly successful On-the-Job Training program for Special Forces Medics could serve as a model in the build up of Civil Affairs soldiers in those technical skills areas such as public works facilities (sewer and water) to provide them with increased technical knowledge. **HOW**: Establish local intern-type agreements with municipal governments in proximity with Special Operations units (example-Fayetteville, NC). This will permit the deploying soldiers a first hand knowledge of systems that aren't easily learned from books or on the site.	**WHAT:** Coordinate with DoD legal that SOCOM has the necessary authority to enter into agreements with local government to conduct intern training (OJT) for Special Operations Personnel. **HOW**: Conduct a legal review.
Review OSS Morale Operations (MO) with the current MISO and CA structures to determine ways to increase team	**WHAT:** The OSS used a variety of psychological warfare techniques in support of tactical OSS operations. SOF should review those OSS techniques to determine how they were used and determine if they are consistent with today's authorities for MISO.	**What:** Coordinate with ASD/SOLIC to determine if new authorities are required to conduct a wider variety of psychological operations to support current SOF operations. If necessary, then assist in the

integration from the planning to execution and synchronization with SF units on a regional orientation.	**HOW:** Review OSS files (after action reports) and compare them with current doctrine and policies to determine if the necessary authorities exist to conduct similar operations. May require some classified study.	development of those required authorities. **HOW**: Review current authorities and modify them as required to ensure the maximum capability of the SOF forces.
Examine existing programs with OSS practices to bring native speakers into the program in order to employ their skills more quickly.	**WHAT**: Review the language skills for recruiting of the OSS to determine how they can be incorporated into existing selection programs. OSS practices also need to be reviewed in reference to the security classification levels that were necessary to perform their duties. **HOW**: Compare the MAVNI and other culture/language based selection programs to how the OSS recruited for language and cultural skills. There should also be consideration given to what level of security classification levels are required to support SOF needs. There are different levels of security needs ranging from basic translation of unclassified documents to integration of High Value Targets (HVT).	**WHAT:** Seek ASD SOLIC, SOLA support in obtaining new authorities or new policies on recruiting uniquely language qualified personnel under MAVNI or other similar programs. **HOW**: SOCOM provides information, studies or reports on language qualified personnel from priority regions or to support the SOCOM Persistent Engagement Program to support new authorities, policies or programs.
Review the OSS structure with current SOF organizations to determine what capabilities require updating.	**WHAT**: The OSS was a "purpose built" organization that focused on a small foot print. A comparison of the OSS and SOF structures would determine if SOF has the necessary capabilities to meet the current challenges. As an example, the OSS work on economic warfare is worthy of examination for SOCOM. **HOW**: Conducted detailed examination of the branches of the OSS and compare them with today's SOCOM organizations to determine what capabilities are missing and how to adapt them in the force.	
Conduct a review of a SF concept of SAF (bolt-ons) structure to enhance the forward deployed SF battalions in order to increase	**WHAT:** OSS was an organization of small elements and could be tailored for an operation. It assembled the necessary elements within the theater, because they were language and culturally capable to support each other quickly. They referred to this as "bolt-on." SOCOM units have organizations that are regionally focused	

capabilities and unit cohesion in regional operations.	and they can be tailored for missions. In the 1960-1970s, SF were organized in their forward deployed units as a structure called Special Action Force (SAF). **HOW:** Review the history and AAR from the 8th and 10th Special Forces Groups with their experiences with SAF elements.	
Review IATF plans to determine other ways to leverage economic tools (follow the money) by considering how the OSS employed their economic warfare organizations.	**WHAT:** OSS had a basic Interagency design with connections to STATE Department, JUSTICE (FBI) and TREASURY in the D.C. area and more limited connection at the operational level normally at the Theater level. The economic warfare approach of the OSS is an area to be further investigated by SOCOM beyond the current "follow the money". **HOW**: Engage the SOCOM IATF to investigate what is currently being done and compare it with how the OSS conducted economic warfare.	
	Resourcing	
Accelerate SOF to Service common acquisitions to reduce duplicative acquisition costs and increase programmatic economies of scale.	**WHAT:** Investigate how to reduce the amount of duplication in the acquisition process in place today in SOF programs. The purpose of this study is to determine if SOCOM needs a more Service-like status for acquisition. **HOW:** Investigate the current authorities, regulations and policy that govern SOCOM acquisition to determine where improvements can be made.	
Concentrate SOF resources on select persistent engagement activities with the intent to better "Manage" the global environment.	**WHAT**: Persistent Engagement is a key program in managing the global environment and SOCOM needs to ensure that it's resources to be flexibility in the use of those funds. **HOW**: Review current funding authorities, policies, and directives that affect Persistent Engagement Activities to ensure efficiencies exist.	

Tailor DOD oversight; manage USSOCOM more as a Special Activity with appropriate funds vice a Service-like entity by reducing numbers of reviews, reports, and decision layers.	**WHAT**: Review all funding sources to determine the oversight requirements and the impact on the availability of funds and evaluate whether SOCOM needs more Service-like responsibilities. **HOW:** Direct review of SOCOM funding to determine ways to reduce oversight or layers of decision making in order to seek relief from unnecessary bureaucracy.	
Empower USSOCOM to operate with funding similar to OSS's un-vouchered to reduce overhead and increase USSOCOM's ability to meet urgent needs.	**WHAT**: Review funding reporting requirements to determine ways to reduce bureaucracy and improve ways to employ the funding operationally rather than reporting or accounting procedures. **HOW:** Direct review of how the OSS was funded and how it accounted for the expenditures, then compare it to the requirements placed on SOCOM today for similar activities in order to seek ways to reduce the overhead.	**WHAT**: OSD, congressional and NCA approval required funding authorities and the oversight to determine how to streamline the number of oversights actions on that funding. **HOW**: Review all oversights actions and compare them to determine how they can be streamlined to reduce amount time necessary for approvals and reporting.
Create a human capital plan to further develop and harness the regional, cultural, and linguistic expertise of our organic SOF operators and enablers.	**WHAT**: SOCOM needs to review its' Human Capital Plan to determine how to maximize the resources available, SOF and non-SOF, DDD, and retired (SOF of Life). **HOW:** Direct a review of the SOCOM Human Capital Plan to determine what deficiencies exist and where the plan can be improved. Examine how a concept of "SOF for Life" to determine how use retired SOF personnel on an as needed bases for regional crisis responses.	
Authorities		
Tailor DOD oversight; manage USSOCOM more	**WHAT:** As a baseline, documentation in a consolidated format is required to illustrate the layers of bureaucracy in reporting	**WHAT**: Majority of work will be to convince DOD and OSD chain of command to support.

as a Special Activity with appropriate funds by reducing numbers of reviews, reports, and decision layers.	mechanisms and requirements for each SOF funding/authorities program. USSOCOM policy branch has an excellent start with their authorities' portal. **HOW**: Each of the Funding Authorities should be reviewed and determine the overlap in reporting and make recommendations on where they can be streamlined.	Congressional approval will be required to reduce the amount of bureaucracy involved in the Special Activities funding. **HOW:** Present findings from SOCOM studies on oversights burdens and layers of bureaucracy that don't contribute to regional solutions to seek relieve from those requirements.
Refocus and enhance 1206/1207/1208 Authorities to support partner nations.	**WHAT**: Currently the funding authorities are a compromise between DoS and DoD, but there needs to be better synchronization of the funding. **HOW**: The funding lines need to be analyzed to simplify their use and reporting procedures.	**WHAT**: Congressional and interagency coordination and approval required to simplify the use and reporting of these funds by SOF personnel. **HOW:** Conduct review of the funding lines and determine where they can be simplified and be more flexible in their use by SOF personnel.
Empower USSOCOM to operate with funding similar to OSS's unvouchered funds in order to reduce overhead and increase ability to meet urgent needs. *Refine roles and responsibilities in synchronizing global operations and develop Joint SOF Doctrine to support.*	**WHAT:** Provide SOCOM with the necessary authority to control the operational funding in a more flexible manner and reduce the amount of oversight on those funds without the loss of accountability of those funds. **HOW:** Review the OSS funding and accountability systems to determine how to utilize that flexibility for SOCOM. The amount of oversight and accountability for SOCOM consumes large amount of time and duplication of effort which should be reduced while preserving fidelity of the funding accountability.	**WHAT**: OSD, congressional and NCA approval required funding authorities and the oversight to determine how to streamline the number of oversights actions on that funding. **HOW**: Review all oversights actions and compare them to determine how they can be streamlined to reduce amount time necessary for approvals and reporting.
Increase authorities and roles in intelligence operations	**WHAT**: Review current intelligence authorities and determine what new authorities are needed. **HOW:** Requires classified discussion.	**WHAT:** OSD, congressional and interagency coordination and approval required for new Intelligence Authorities. **HOW:** Review findings from both unclassified and classified studies

		to determine deficiencies and propose
Refine roles and responsibilities in synchronizing global operations and **develop Joint SOF Doctrine** to support.	Current Joint SOF Doctrine JP 3-05 (dated 1998, and revised in 2003) is outdated and requires a rewrite	Coordination with services and DOD required.

Annex B: Innovation Workshop

This annex is a synopsis of the JSOU After-Action-Report for the 16 November 2010 OSS Innovation Workshop directed by Admiral Olson. This annex places into context the scope of work the USSOCOM study members were tasked to complete. It also highlights the compressed timeline that followed this workshop which culminated with the symposium held in early January 2011.

DISCUSSION:

a. USSOCOM Commander, Admiral Eric T. Olson, commissioned a series of four Innovation Workshops to encourage creative and imaginative thinking on the part of the USSOCOM J-code staff. This Workshop, third in the series, focused on the Office of Strategic Services (OSS) and was intended to spark the participants' imagination and interest in determining which OSS practices and procedures might serve as a model to apply in the future of SOF. Workshop participants will contribute to a follow-up study to examine the OSS experience and potential applications. The study will concentrate on four topics: Selection Process, Organization, Resourcing, and Authorities. Outcomes from this total effort will influence the commander's testimony, as well as USSOCOM doctrine, and policy recommendations. The study will conclude with a seminar on 11-12 January 2011, MacDill AFB, to validate and prioritize recommendations to be presented to Admiral Olson.

b. The Workshop included presentations by Admiral Olson and Dr. Nancy Collins, Columbia University, and a series of discussion topics. The blending of the presentations and discussions resulted in the desired outcome for the study.

c. Observations:

1) Admiral Olson addressed three key points in his welcome:

a) He used the —warrior-diplomats" concept (3D warrior) to move into his main point: a discussion of the SOF worldwide footprint. He showed a series of nightly world maps that demonstrated through the use of lights to indicate where SOF is and needs to be. However, he stated we are not prepared to be in those countries that are in the dark. The Admiral said SOF will be successful by engaging with small teams who can operate with the wits and have the authority to do so.

b) He charged the group to —be imaginative and get outside your organizational cocoons and be creative..." He strongly suggested that this effort at —initiative of thought" could influence the future of USSOCOM.

c) His last point referred to how USSOCOM should be viewed. The Admiral reminded the assembly that Dr. Dave Kilcullen, an Australian SOF expert, believes USSOCOM should have been named —Strategic" and not —Special". This simple name change reflects a difference between levels of employment of the forces. He referenced a War College paper written by LTG (ret) Jerry Boykin that also called for the name to be Strategic Services Command. Admiral Olson believes SOF are and should be strategic assets.

2) Dr. Maher introduced the Workshop and described the project scope which includes this workshop, an attendant study, a concluding seminar, and a report with recommendations to the Commander. The Workshop marked the beginning of the study

effort that will conclude with a seminar 11-12 January 2011. The study will focus on four topics: Selection Process, Organization, Resourcing, and Enabling Authorities. The seminar will feature the final validation and priority ranking of the study recommendations which have the potential to influence the future of SOF.

    3) JSOU Senior Fellow, Mr. Jeff Nelson, set the conditions for approaching the study with a review of some elements of critical thinking, a discussion of hindrances to critical thinking, and examples were given to illustrate how they can affect operational decisions. To further emphasize these points, Mr. Nelson offered a set of operational terms to show linkage and to stimulate thinking about what the USSOCOM J-code staff knows and doesn't know about operational terms and terminology.

    4) Dr. Nancy Walbridge Collins, professor of contemporary history at Columbia University, was the keynote speaker for the Workshop. She analyzed the OSS model and its potential applicability for USSOCOM.

    a) Dr. Collins outlined some of the historical links between OSS and USSOCOM, tracing the ways in which OSS may be considered a precursor organization to USSOCOM, and how this earlier model could be utilized as a historical force to propel future changes.

    b) She delineated some of the challenges/obstacles that could arise from these efforts, especially noting well-established and direct linkages between the OSS model and CIA history, which have created parallel narratives and ripple effects on the SOF story.

    c) Dr. Collins provided a brief outline of OSS origins/development/dissolution and emphasized characteristics of OSS that could serve as sparks for workshop dialogue:

    i. OSS was established as a *strategic* operation, fusing operations and intelligence at all levels, in a highly adaptive and creative environment

    ii. Afforded exceptional *authorities,* which ensured wide *latitude* and maximum *flexibility*

    iii. Operated with *both centralized and decentralized* activities, led by a charismatic leader who established high standards and then expected deputies/ operatives/ analysts to take on great individual responsibility for decision-making

    iv. Emphasized a *culture of experts*, with focus on specific/detailed context knowledge

    v. Recruited individuals *for what they already knew*; there was little time for training; focused on industry civilians who brought in elite networks and refugees, émigrés, and immigrants who offered in-depth cultural awareness and native language capabilities

    vi. Operated with *small footprints,* without bells and whistles, and called on individuals who had considerable appetite for calculated risks and sophisticated cognitive skill

    vii. Focused on *integrating* capabilities, in response to emergency conditions rather than creating new functions

    d) Dr. Collins then addressed the potential problem of OSS nostalgia, to avoid any suggestion that there was a SOF utopia in the past. She highlighted a few OSS challenges during WWII, notably:

i. Intense rivalry between OSS and other defense/intelligence agencies over resources, authorities, and manpower

ii. Lack of inherited/existing infrastructure for their work, which resulted in some spectacular operational failures

iii. Inability to institutionalize authorities and structures before the death of President Roosevelt in 1945

e) And to underscore some of the challenges in the applicability of the model today, Dr. Collins noted a few of the key environmental differences:

i. The *total war environment* of WWII, with national mobilization, drafts, and domestic near-unanimity and contributions

ii. Nearly everything was *innovative/new*: no barnacles to scrape/ship had not yet been built; bureaucracy was not yet formed, much less entrenched

iii. *Exceptionally close civil-military relations*, including deep and knowledgeable support of OSS by key Washington policymakers

f) In conclusion, Dr. Collins posed two questions about the potential applicability of the OSS Model:

i. Could it serve as a potential *heritage touchstone*; inspiration for today's SOF warrior, by promoting focus on understanding and the values of finesse, focus, persistence, flexibility, creativity, leadership and wisdom?

ii. Could it serve as a means to enhance USSOCOM's mission as a *strategic services* command?

5) The Workshop discussion focused on three discussion topics on the areas of Understanding, Small Footprint, and Authorities.

a) Understanding: This topic provided for an initial free flow of ideas between the participants and featured a Question and Answer exchange with Dr. Collins. Some key discussion ideas were:

i. Influence and action are part of the strategic end states. These are shaping ideas that are better ways to do things.

ii. OSS may be a good business practice to be examined, but the military is good at creating legends and we need to be careful of not falling into the trap of blindly following the ―mythology of the OSS."

iii. Question of how to leverage patriotic civilians to engage in military operations and understand what authorities are available to engage them.

iv. The battlefield landscape is changing from rural to urban to electronic. We need to understand how to prepare our ―snake-eaters" for this new environment.

v. There is a need to understand space and cyber space environments.

vi. Understanding current authorities and forecast new authority requirements. One comment from the participants was ―keep me at the LOR level" as far as advice from legal counselors.

b) Small Footprint:

i. USSOCOM headquarters is not prepared to be flexible in organization or equipment.

ii. OSS Command and Control was one of maximum flexibility. The farther from the HQ, the more flexibility the mission had. Innovation and creativity were the hallmarks for success.

iii. The status of SOF for Life was discussed and questioned.

      iv. OSS learned that they needed to be there (in the area of operations) earlier in their operations. It takes time to build relationships and to execute operations.

      v. SF is learning that 12 may not be the correct number (for a team) and augmentation may be required.

      vi. Individual career-track requirements hurt SOF continuity.

  c) Authorities:

      i. ADM Olson did not want to use Afghanistan as a model for review.

      ii. A new mindset must be ―how to do this" not one of ―it can't be done."

      iii. There is a need for layered authorities to support the mission.

      iv. There is need for authority for teams to manage operational funds, like the OSS was able to do.

      v. Department of State has some authority to hire under Title 5 US Code, Section 3161 to hire select experts for one year terms of service; the Admiral was interested to learn more about this authority.

      vi. More needs to be done with authorities to understand what needs to be changed.

CONCLUSION:

  a. ADM Olson closed the workshop and provided some final thoughts:

  1) The 9-11 Commission had only one recommendation that was not implemented. The recommendation had to do with USSOCOM becoming the lead organization for paramilitary operations for the U.S. government. (CIA currently is the lead organization.)

  2) Since 9-11, we still need to practice ―Shoot, move and communicate." We are better at shooting, mobility is improved, and our communication capability is tremendous. However, we need to add, ―Understand" to this fundamental expression of skills. We need to be prepared for the ―lights out" portions of the map.

  3) In his last comment he noted that we spent huge energy on the bad guys but we need to spend more energy on knowing who the good guys are.

  b. JSOU will collect detailed notes and circulate to USSOCOM Components and other stakeholders to prepare a study and recommendations for the 11-12 January 2011 seminar at MacDill AFB.

Annex C: OSS Innovation Workshop and OSS Study Participants

CDR Janet Lomax	USSOCOM J1
Jennifer Nevius	USSOCOM J1
Nick Pultorak	USSOCOM J2 CIO
Wade Clare	USSOCOM J3X
Brian Sweeney	USSOCOM J39
Leonardo Yuque	USSOCOM J51
Bob Berry	USSOCOM J51
John Bone	USSOCOM J53
Steven Kline	USSOCOM J55
Chris McNulty	USSOCOM J7/9
Robert Hyde	USSOCOM J7/9
LTC Eric Shwedo	USSOCOM J7/9
Mark Truluck	USSOCOM J7/9
Rick Lamb	USSOCOM IATF
Chris O'Connor	USSOCOM IATF/DOS
Aaron Thompson	USSOCOM IATF/FBI
Jim Ladd	USSOCOM IATF
Camilo Guerro	JMISC-RF
Jamie Charlton	USSOCOM JMISC
CAPT Charles Lockett	USSOCOM
MAJ Lewis Powers	CENTCOM J33
COL Louie M. Banks, III	USASOC
Lt Col Steven Gregg	ACC

Annex D: Recommended OSS Reading List

This list serves as basic guide for literature and recommending readings that are relevant to the historical study of the OSS and its impact on the intelligence community, the Central Intelligence Agency, and Special Operations Forces.

Robert Hayden Alcorn, *No Bugles for Spies: Tales of the OSS* (New York: D. McKay Co., 1962).

Richard Aldrich, *Intelligence and the War Against Japan: Britain, America and the Politics of Secret Service* (Cambridge: Cambridge University Press, 1999).

Stewart Alsop and Thomas Braden, *Sub Rosa: The OSS and American Espionage* (New York: Reynal & Hitchcock, 1946).

Christopher M. Andrew, *For the President's Eyes Only: Secret Intelligence and the American Presidency from Washington to Bush* (New York: Harper Collins Publishers, 1995).

Aaron Bank, *From OSS to Green Berets: The Birth of Special Forces* (Novato, CA: Presidio, 1986).

Colin Beavan, *Operation Jedburgh: D-Day and America's First Shadow War* (New York: Viking,   2006).

Howard Blue, *Words at War: World War II Era Radio Drama and the Postwar Broadcasting Industry Blacklist* (Lanham: Scarecrow Press, 2002).

Anthony Cave Brown, *The Last Hero: Wild Bill Donovan* (New York: Times Books, 1982).

Anthony Cave Brown, *The Secret War Report of the OSS* (New York: Berkeley Pub. Corp, 1976).

David K. E. Bruce, edited by Nelson D. Lankford, *OSS Against the Reich* (Kent, OH: Kent State   University Press, 1991).

John W. Brunner, *OSS Weapons* (Williamstown, NJ: Phillips Publications, 1994).

Roger Burlingame, *Don't Let Them Scare You: The Life and Times of Elmer Davis* (Philadelphia: Lippincott, 1961).

William J. Casey, *The Secret War Against Hitler* (Washington, DC: Regnery Gateway: 1988).

George C. Chalou, *The Secrets War: The Office of Strategic Services in World War II* (Washington, DC: National Archives and Records Administration, 1992).

Ray S. Cline, *The CIA: Reality vs. Myth* (Washington: Acropolis Books, 1982).

William Egan Colby and Peter Forbath, *Honorable Men: My Life in the CIA* (New York: Simon and Schuster, 1978).

Max Corvo, *The O.S.S. In Italy, 1942-1945: A Personal Memoir* (New York: Praeger, 1990).

Richard W. Cutler, *I Came, I Saw, I Wrote: A Risk-Takers Life in Law, Espionage, Community Service,   Start-Ups and Writing* (Milwaukee, WI: Richard W. Cutler, 2010).

Arthur B. Darling, *The Central Intelligence Agency: An Instrument of Government, to 1950* (United   States: Historical Staff, Central Intelligence Agency, 1989).

Helias Doundoulakis, *I Was Trained to Be a Spy: A True Life Story* (Philadelphia: Xlibris, 2008).

Allen Welsh Dulles, *The Craft of Intelligence* (New York: Harper & Row, 1963).

Allen Welsh Dulles, *The Secret Surrender* (New York: Harper & Row, 1966).

Allen Welsh Dulles, with Neal H. Petersen, *From Hitler's Doorstep: The Wartime Intelligence Reports of Allen Dulles, 1942-1945* (University Park, PA: Pennsylvania State University Press, 1996).

Richard Dunlop, *Behind Japanese Lines, with the OSS in Burma* (Chicago: Rand McNally, 1979).

Richard Dunlop, *Donovan, America's Master Spy* (Chicago: Rand McNally, 1982).

Captain Charles Fenn, *At the Dragon's Gate: With the OSS in the Far East* (Annapolis: Naval Institute Press, 2004).

David J. Ferrier, *ONI and OSS in World War II* (Washington, DC: Navy & Marine Corps WWII Commemorative Committee, Navy Office of Information, 1995).

Corey Ford, *Donovan of OSS* (Boston: Little, Brown, 1970).

Kirk Ford, *OSS and the Yugoslav Resistance, 1943-1945* (College Station: Texas A & M University Press, 1992).

James L. Gilbert and John Patrick Finnegan, *U.S. Army Signals Intelligence in World War II: A Documentary History* (Washington D.C.: Center of Military History, United States Army, 1993).

Roger Hall, *You're Stepping on My Cloak and Dagger* (New York: W.W. Norton, 1957).

Jürgen Heideking, Christof Mauch, and Marc Frey, *American Intelligence and the German Resistance to Hitler: A Documentary History* (Boulder, Colo.: Westview Press, 1996).

F.H. Hinsley, E.E. Thomas, C.F.G. Ransom, R. C. Knight, C.A.G. Simkins, and Michael Howard, *British Intelligence in the Second World War* (New York: Cambridge University Press, 1979).

Maurice Isserman, *Which Side Were You On?: The American Communist Party During the Second World War* (Middletown, CT.: Wesleyan University Press, 1982).

Jay Jakub, *Spies and Saboteurs: Anglo-American Collaboration and Rivalry in Human Intelligence Collection and Special Operations, 1940-45* (St. Martin's Press, 1999).

Rhodri Jeffreys-Jones, *Cloak and Dollar: A History of American Secret Intelligence* (New

Haven: Yale University Press, 2002).

Gary Kamiya, *Shadow Knights: The Secret War Against Hitler* (New York: Simon & Schuster, 2010).

I. L. Kandel, *The Impact of the War Upon American Education* (Chapel Hill: Univ. of North Carolina   Press, 1949).

Barry Katz, *Foreign Intelligence: Research and Analysis in the Office of Strategic Services, 1942-1945* (Cambridge, MA: Harvard University Press, 1989).

Louis E. Keefer, *Scholars in Foxholes: The Story of the Army Specialized Training Program in World War II* (Jefferson, NC: McFarland & Co., 1988).

Sherman Kent, *Strategic Intelligence for American World Policy* (Princeton, NJ: Princeton Univ. Press, 1949).

Marcia Christoff Kurapovna, *Shadows on the Mountain: The Allies, the Resistance, and the Rivalries   That Doomed WWII Yugoslavia* (Hoboken, NJ: Wiley, 2010).

William L. Langer, *In and Out of the Ivory Tower* (New York: N. Watson Academic Publications, 1977).

Nelson D. Lankford, *The Last American Aristocrat: The Biography of David K.E. Bruce, 1898-1977* (Boston: Little, Brown, 1996).

Clayton D. Laurie, *The Propaganda Warriors: America's Crusade Against Nazi Germany* (Lawrence, KS: University Press of Kansas, 1996).

William M. Leary, *The Central Intelligence Agency, History and Documents* (University, AL: University of Alabama Press, 1984).

Wilmarth S. Lewis, *One Man's Education* (New York: Knopf, 1967).

Franklin Lindsay, *Beacons in the Night: With the OSS and Tito's Partisans in Wartime Yugoslavia* (Stanford, CA: Stanford University Press, 1993).

Eugene Liptak, *Office of Strategic Services, 1942-45: The World War II Origins of the CIA* (Oxford: New York, 2009).

Elizabeth P. McIntosh, *Sisterhood of Spies: The Women of the OSS* (Annapolis, MD: Naval Institute Press, 1998).

H. Keith Melton, *OSS Special Weapons & Equipment: Spy Devices of W.W. II* (New York: Sterling,   1991).

Ludwell Lee Montague, *General Walter Bedell Smith as Director of Central Intelligence, October 1950-February 1953* (University Park, PA: Pennsylvania State University Press, 1992).

J. Robert Moskin, *Mr. Truman's War: The Final Victories of World War II and the Birth of the*

Postwar World (Lawrence, KS: University Press of Kansas, 2002).

Wayne Nelson, *A Spy's Diary of World War II: Inside the OSS with an American Agent in Europe* (Jefferson, NC: McFarland, 2009).

Patrick K. O'Donnell, *Operatives, Spies, and Saboteurs: The Unknown Story of the Men and Women of World War II's OSS* Free Press, 2004).

Patrick K. O'Donnell, *The Brenner Assignment: The Untold Story of the Most Daring Spy Mission of World War II* (Cambridge, MA: Da Capo, 2008).

G. J. A. O'Toole, *Honorable Treachery: A History of U.S. Intelligence, Espionage, and Covert Action from the American Revolution to the CIA* (New York: Atlantic Monthly Press, 1991).

Wyman H. Packard, *A Century of U.S. Naval Intelligence* (Washington, DC: Office of Naval Intelligence: Naval Historical Center, 1996).

Joseph E. Persico, *Piercing the Reich: The Penetration of Nazi Germany by American Secret Agents During World War II* (New York: Viking Press, 1979).

Joseph E. Persico, *Casey: From the OSS to the CIA* (New York, N.Y: Viking, 1990).

Joseph E. Persico, *Roosevelt's Secret War: FDR and World War II Espionage* (New York: Random House, 2001).

Daniel C. Pinck, Geoffrey M.T. Jones, and Charles T. Pinck, *Stalking the History of the Office of Strategic Services: An OSS Bibliography* (Boston, MA: OSS, Donovan Press, 2000).

John Ranelagh, *The Agency: The Rise and Decline of the CIA* (New York: Simon and Schuster, 1986).

Harry Howe Ransom, *Central Intelligence and National Security, The Intelligence Establishment* (Cambridge: Harvard University Press, 1970).

David Reynolds, *The Creation of the Anglo-American Alliance, 1937-41: A Study in Competitive Co-Operation* (Chapel Hill: University of North Carolina Press, 1982).

David Reynolds, *From Munich to Pearl Harbor: Roosevelt's America and the Origins of the Second World War* (Chicago: Ivan R. Dee, 2001).

Mark Riebling, *Wedge: The Secret War Between the FBI and CIA* (New York: A.A. Knopf, 1994).

Kermit Roosevelt, *War Report of the OSS (Office of Strategic Services)* (New York: Walker, 1976).

Barry M. Rubin, *Secrets of State: The State Department and the Struggle over U.S. Foreign Policy* (New York: Oxford, 1985).

David F. Rudgers, *Creating the Secret State: The Origins of the Central Intelligence Agency,*

1943-1947 (Lawrence: University Press of Kansas, 2000).

Arthur M. Schlesinger, *A Life in the Twentieth Century: Innocent Beginnings, 1917-1950* (Boston, MA: Houghton Mifflin, 2000).

David F. Schmitz, *Henry L. Stimson: The First Wise Man* (Wilmington, DE: Scholarly Resources, 2000).

Bradley F. Smith, *The Shadow Warriors: O.S.S. and the Origins of the CIA* (New York: Basic Books, 1983).

Bradley F. Smith and Elena Agarossi, *Operation Sunrise: The Secret Surrender* (New York, NY: Basic Books, 1979).

R. Harris Smith, *OSS: The Secret History of America's First Central Intelligence Agency* (Berkeley: University of California Press, 1972).

Phyllis L. Soybel, *A Necessary Relationship: The Development of Anglo-American Cooperation in Naval Intelligence* (Westport, CT.: Praeger, 2005).

Donald Paul Steury, *The Intelligence War* (New York: Metro Books, 2000).

Phil Swearngin, *Secret Heroes* (Scotts Valley, CA: CreateSpace, 2009).

Marianna Torgovnick, *The War Complex: World War II in Our Time* (Chicago: University of Chicago Press, 2005).

Thomas F. Troy, *Donovan and the CIA: A History of the Establishment of the Central Intelligence Agency* (Frederick, Md.: Aletheia Books, 1981).

Thomas F. Troy, *Wild Bill and Intrepid: Donovan, Stephenson, and the Origin of CIA* (New Haven: Yale University Press, 1996).

U.S. Department of State, *Foreign Relations of the United States, 1945-1950, Emergence of the Intelligence Establishment* (Washington, DC: Government Printing Office, 1996).

Douglas C. Waller, *Wild Bill Donovan* (New York: Free Press, 2010).

Michael Warner, *The Office of Strategic Services: America's First Intelligence Agency* (Washington, DC: Public Affairs, Central Intelligence Agency, 2002).

Robin W. Winks, *Cloak & Gown: Scholars in the Secret War, 1939-1961* (New York: Morrow, 1987).

Maochun Yu, *OSS in China: Prelude to Cold War* (New Haven: Yale University Press, 1996).

www.ingramcontent.com/pod-product-compliance
Lightning Source LLC
Chambersburg PA
CBHW080851010626
R18375900001B/R183759PG45790CBX00013B/25